MYSTERIES OF ISTANBUL

33 HIDDEN STORIES FROM A SACRED CITY

DAVID PETAULT

CONTENTS

FOREWORD

I am happy you chose to read "Mysteries of Istanbul." It's a collection of short stories, mysteries, and folklore from yet another one of my favorite cities in the world. I hope these tales will help you capture the essence of Istanbul, from its ancient legends to its enduring mysteries.

Each story offers a unique glimpse into the people, places, and events that make Istanbul so captivating.

Whether you're a history enthusiast or just love a good story, I hope you enjoy exploring the magic of Istanbul through these pages as much as I enjoyed gathering the stories and writing them.

David Petault

A BRIEF HISTORY OF ISTANBUL

Istanbul, a city straddling two continents, has a history as rich and layered as the civilizations that have called it home. From its humble beginnings as a Greek colony to its current status as a global metropolis, Istanbul's story is one of constant transformation and enduring significance.

The city's origins date back to around 660 BCE when Greek colonists from Megara, led by King Byzas, established a settlement called Byzantium on the European side of the Bosphorus Strait.

This strategic location, controlling the passage between the Black Sea and the Mediterranean, ensured the city's importance from its very inception.

For centuries, Byzantium remained a relatively small but prosperous city-state, weathering invasions and changing allegiances. Its fortunes changed dramatically in 330 CE when Roman Emperor Constantine the Great chose it as the new capital of the Roman Empire. Renamed Constantinople, the city was lavishly rebuilt and expanded, becoming the center of Christian civilization in the East.

Under Byzantine rule, Constantinople flourished as a center of art, culture, and learning. The construction of the Hagia Sophia in 537 CE, with its massive dome and intricate mosaics, symbolized the city's grandeur and spiritual importance. The city's population grew, its defenses were strengthened, and it became known as the "Queen of Cities."

However, Constantinople's position as the capital of the Christian world made it a target for numerous invasions. The city withstood sieges by Persians, Arabs, Bulgars, and Russians, its massive walls proving a formidable defense. The Fourth Crusade in 1204 CE saw the city sacked by Western Christians, a blow from which the Byzantine Empire never fully recovered.

The Ottoman Turks, who had been gradually conquering Byzantine territories, finally laid siege to Constantinople in 1453. Under the leadership of Sultan Mehmed II, they breached the city walls on May 29, marking the end of the Byzantine Empire and the birth of Ottoman Constantinople.

The Ottomans swiftly set about transforming the city. Mehmed II declared it the new capital of his empire, and the Hagia Sophia was converted into a mosque. The city was repopulated with people from across the Ottoman territories, creating a diverse, multicultural metropolis. Grand new mosques, including the Sultanahmet (Blue) Mosque, were built, rivaling the splendor of the Byzantine monuments.

Under Ottoman rule, Istanbul (as it was increasingly known, though Constantinople remained the official name) entered a new golden age. It became the center of a vast empire stretching from Hungary to Egypt, from the Caucasus to Algeria. The city's population soared, making it one of the largest in the world. The Grand Bazaar, still one of the world's largest covered markets, was expanded, symbolizing the city's importance as a trade hub.

The 16th and 17th centuries saw Istanbul at the height of its power and influence. Ottoman architecture reached its zenith under the great architect Sinan, whose works like the Süleymaniye Mosque complex still dominate the city's skyline. The city was a melting pot of cultures, with Turkish, Greek, Armenian, Jewish, and many other communities contributing to its vibrant social fabric.

However, as the Ottoman Empire began to decline in the 18th and 19th centuries, so too did the fortunes of its capital. The empire's weakness was exploited by European powers, and Istanbul found itself increasingly influenced by Western culture and politics. The Tanzimat reforms of the 19th century saw attempts to modernize the city, with the introduction of trams, modern universities, and Western-style architecture.

The final years of Ottoman rule were marked by political instability and economic hardship. World War I proved disastrous for the empire, and following its defeat, Istanbul was occupied by Allied forces in 1918. This occupation lasted until 1923, when the Turkish War of Independence, led by Mustafa Kemal Atatürk, resulted in the formation of the Turkish Republic.

In a significant break with the past, Atatürk moved the capital to Ankara, ending Istanbul's status as an imperial capital after 1600 years. The city's name was officially changed to Istanbul in 1930, though this had been the common Turkish name for centuries.

Despite losing its capital status, Istanbul remained Turkey's economic and cultural powerhouse. The mid-20th century saw rapid industrialization and urbanization, with the city's population exploding as people moved from rural areas in search of work. This growth led to the expansion of the city on both the European and Asian sides, with new neighborhoods springing up rapidly, often in an unplanned manner.

The construction of the first bridge over the Bosphorus in 1973 physically linked the European and Asian sides of the city, symbolizing Istanbul's role as a bridge between continents. This was followed by a second bridge in 1988 and a third in 2016, along with an undersea tunnel, facilitating the city's expansion and integration.

The latter half of the 20th century and the beginning of the 21st have seen Istanbul transform into a global city. Its population has grown to over 15 million, making it one of the world's largest urban areas. The city has become a major tourist destination, with millions of visitors each year coming to experience its historical sites, vibrant culture, and unique position between East and West.

Istanbul's economy has diversified and grown significantly, becoming a key player in finance, manufacturing, and technology sectors. The city's skyline has been transformed with modern skyscrapers and ambitious development projects, sometimes controversially encroaching on historical areas.

However, this rapid growth and development have not been without challenges. Traffic congestion, environmental concerns, and the strain on urban infrastructure are ongoing issues. The city also sits on a major fault line, with the ever-present risk of a major earthquake looming over its future plans.

Culturally, Istanbul continues to be a city of contrasts and diversity. It's a place where centuries-old mosques and churches stand alongside modern art galleries and nightclubs. Traditional bazaars coexist with gleaming shopping malls, and ancient traditions blend with contemporary lifestyles.

The city's strategic importance remains as relevant today as it was when King Byzas founded his colony. Istanbul is a key link between Europe and Asia, a crucial shipping route, and a major player in regional politics. Its position as a cultural and economic bridge between East and West continues to shape its identity and influence.

As Istanbul moves further into the 21st century, it faces both opportunities and challenges. Climate change, urban planning, preservation of historical heritage, and maintaining social cohesion in a rapidly changing world are all issues the city must grapple with. Yet, if history is any guide, Istanbul will adapt and evolve as it has done for millennia.

From Byzantium to Constantinople to Istanbul, this city has been at the center of world events for over two and a half millennia. It has been a capital of empires, a melting pot of cultures, and a symbol of both division and unity between East and West. As it continues to grow and change, Istanbul remains a city where history is not just remembered but lived, where the past and future coexist in a unique and dynamic present.

The story of Istanbul is far from over. As it has done throughout its long and storied history, the city continues to reinvent itself, facing the future while never forgetting its past. In its streets and squares, in its monuments and in its people, Istanbul carries the legacy of its many pasts into an exciting and uncertain future, remaining as it has always been - a city like no other.

MYSTERIES OF ISTANBUL

1

THE MAIDEN'S TOWER

The Maiden's Tower rises from the Bosphorus Strait, a solitary sentinel against the backdrop of Istanbul's skyline. Its weathered stones have witnessed centuries of history, but none so poignant as the tale of a father's love and the futility of fighting fate.

In days long past, when empires rose and fell along these shores, a powerful emperor ruled the land. He was a man of great wealth and influence, but his most treasured possession was his only daughter. The princess grew into a young woman of exceptional beauty and wit, adored by all who knew her.

On the princess's eighteenth birthday, the emperor arranged for a lavish celebration. Soothsayers and fortune tellers from across the realm gathered to offer blessings and predictions for the princess's future. As the night wore on, one ancient mystic approached the throne. Her eyes, clouded with age, seemed to peer beyond the veil of time itself.

The old woman's pronouncement chilled the emperor to his core: his beloved daughter would die from a snake bite before her next birthday.

Driven by fear and desperate to thwart this grim prophecy, the emperor devised a plan. He would build a sanctuary where no snake could reach his daughter. He commissioned the finest archi-tects and stonemasons in the land to construct a tower in the middle of the Bosphorus Strait.

For months, workers toiled day and night. The tower slowly emerged from the waters, its foundation anchored to a tiny rocky islet. As it grew taller, it became a source of curiosity for the people of the city. Rumors swirled about its purpose, but few knew the truth.

When the tower was complete, the emperor moved his daughter into her new home. The princess's quarters were luxurious, with every comfort she could desire. Windows offered breathtaking views of the city and the strait, while below, the waters lapped at the tower's base, forming a natural moat no snake could cross.

The emperor visited his daughter often, rowing across the strait in a small boat. He brought her books, musical instruments, and art supplies to pass the time. The princess painted seascapes, wrote poetry, and composed melodies inspired by the rhythms of the waves.

Days turned to weeks, and weeks to months. The princess remained safe in her watery fortress, but she grew restless. She missed the gardens of the palace, the bustle of the city streets, and the company of people her own age. Her only visitors were her father and the servants who brought supplies.

As her nineteenth birthday approached, the emperor's fears began to subside. He had outwitted fate, protected his daughter from harm. In a moment of weakness, he decided to allow a small celebration in the tower.

On the morning of her birthday, the emperor arrived with a beautiful basket of exotic fruits as a gift for his daughter. The fruits had been carefully inspected, their skins polished to a shine. Little did he know that nestled among the colorful bounty, a tiny snake slumbered, having found the perfect hiding spot.

The princess was overjoyed at the gift. As she reached into the basket, fate finally caught up with her. The snake, startled from its sleep, lashed out and sank its fangs into her hand. Within moments, the princess collapsed.

· · ·

Devastated, the emperor realized the futility of his efforts. Despite all his power and resources, he could not change what was destined to be. The tower, meant to be a sanctuary, became a monument to his daughter's memory.

From that day forward, the structure was known as the Maiden's Tower. It stood as a reminder that fate has a way of finding us, no matter how we try to hide. Over the centuries, the tower served many purposes - a lighthouse, a quarantine station, a defense post - but it never lost its connection to the legend that gave it its name.

Today, visitors to Istanbul can see the Maiden's Tower still standing in the Bosphorus. Its walls no longer imprison a princess, but instead welcome guests who come to dine in its restaurant or enjoy the panoramic views. And as the sun sets over the city, painting the waters in gold and crimson, one might imagine the ghost of a young woman gazing out from the tower's windows, finally free to admire the beauty of the city she loved.

The legend of the Maiden's Tower speaks to universal themes: a parent's love, the desire to protect those we care about, and the ultimate uncertainty of life. It reminds us that while we cannot control every aspect of our fate, we can choose how we face it. The princess, though confined, made the most of her circumstances, finding beauty and creativity in her unusual home.

In the end, the tale is not just about death, but about how we live. The emperor's attempts to shield his daughter from life's risks ultimately could not prevent the inevitable. Perhaps, had she been allowed to live fully in the world, she might have learned to recognize and avoid dangers on her own.

.   .   .

The story also reflects the unique character of Istanbul itself - a city where East meets West, where ancient tales blend with modern life, and where the boundary between land and sea is ever-shifting. The Maiden's Tower, straddling two continents, embodies this liminal nature.

As with many legends, the story of the Maiden's Tower has evolved over time. Some versions claim it was built by an ancient Greek king, others attribute it to a Byzantine emperor. In some tellings, the princess is saved by her lover, who disguises himself as a doctor to reach her. These variations speak to the fluid nature of oral tradition and the way stories adapt to reflect the values and desires of different eras.

Regardless of the specific details, the core of the story remains a powerful meditation on love, fate, and the human desire to control the uncontrollable. It continues to captivate visitors to Istanbul, adding another layer to the city's rich cultural landscape.

The Maiden's Tower serves as a physical link between past and present, a tangible reminder of the stories that shape our understanding of the world. As long as it stands in the waters of the Bosphorus, the legend of the ill-fated princess will continue to be told, pondered, and reinterpreted by new generations.

2

HEZARFEN AHMED ÇELEBI

The sun had barely risen over the Bosphorus when Hezarfen Ahmed Çelebi climbed the winding stairs of Galata Tower. It was a crisp morning in 1632, and the city was just beginning to stir. Hezarfen's heart raced, not from the climb, but from anticipation. Today, he would attempt what many deemed impossible.

. . .

For years, Hezarfen had been obsessed with the idea of human flight. He'd spent countless hours studying birds, analyzing their wing structures and flight patterns. In his workshop, hidden away in a quiet corner of Istanbul, he'd constructed wings of his own design - a wooden frame covered with thinly stretched leather, light enough to be lifted by the wind yet sturdy enough to support a man's weight.

As he reached the top of the tower, Hezarfen paused to catch his breath. The view from here never failed to amaze him. The city sprawled out before him, a maze of minarets, domes, and terra-cotta roofs. Across the strait, he could see his target: Üsküdar, on the Asian side of the city. The distance seemed both vast and tantalizing.

Hezarfen wasn't the first to dream of flight. Stories of men attempting to soar like birds dated back centuries. But where others had failed, often with tragic consequences, Hezarfen believed he had found the key. His design incorporated elements he'd observed in nature, combined with principles of physics he'd studied meticulously.

As he strapped on his wings, a small crowd gathered below. Word of his attempt had spread, drawing curious onlookers and skeptics alike. Some called him a visionary; others, a madman. Hezarfen paid them no mind. His focus was solely on the task ahead.

With a deep breath, Hezarfen stepped to the edge of the tower. The wind whipped around him, tugging at his clothes and his improvised wings. For a moment, doubt crept in. What if he was wrong? What if this was nothing more than an elaborate form of suicide?

. . .

But then he thought of all the nights he'd spent perfecting his design, all the failed attempts and minor breakthroughs. He thought of the birds he'd watched so intently, marveling at their effortless mastery of the air. And he thought of the stories yet to be written - of a world where humans could soar above the earth, free from its constraints.

With a shout that was part battle cry, part prayer, Hezarfen leapt from the tower.

For a heart-stopping moment, he plummeted. The ground rushed up to meet him, and the gasps of the crowd below reached his ears. But then, miraculously, the wings caught the air. Hezarfen felt himself lifted, buoyed by currents he'd only theorized about until now.

He was flying.

The sensation was unlike anything he'd ever experienced. The city shrank beneath him as he glided over rooftops and courtyards. People stopped in their tracks, pointing and shouting in disbelief. Hezarfen barely noticed them. His entire being was focused on maintaining his trajectory, making minute adjustments to his wings to catch the most favorable winds.

As he crossed over the Bosphorus, Hezarfen felt a surge of elation. He was doing it - truly doing it. The waters below sparkled in the morning sun, and for a moment, he allowed himself to imagine a future where this view would be commonplace, where the skies would be as busy as the streets.

But reality soon reasserted itself. The flight was taxing, requiring every ounce of Hezarfen's strength and concentration. As he approached the shores of Üsküdar, he began to look for a suitable landing spot. His arms ached from the strain of controlling the wings, and he knew he couldn't stay aloft much longer.

With a mixture of relief and regret, Hezarfen aimed for an open square. As the ground rushed up to meet him, he braced for impact. The landing was far from graceful - a tumbling roll that left him bruised and breathless - but he was alive. More than that, he had achieved the impossible.

As he lay on the ground, staring up at the sky he'd just traversed, Hezarfen began to laugh. It started as a chuckle and grew into a full-bodied roar of triumph and disbelief. He'd done it. He'd flown.

News of Hezarfen's feat spread quickly through the city. By nightfall, it seemed all of Istanbul was talking about the man who'd flown across the Bosphorus. Some hailed him as a genius, a pioneer who'd ushered in a new age of possibility. Others were more skeptical, claiming it must have been some sort of trick or illusion.

For Hezarfen, the reality of his accomplishment was still sinking in. As he made his way back to his workshop, wings in tow, he was already thinking of improvements, refinements to his design that could make future flights longer, more stable.

. . .

But not everyone was impressed by Hezarfen's achievement. The Ottoman Sultan Murad IV, known for his volatile temper and suspicious nature, saw the flight as a potential threat. If a man could fly over the Bosphorus, what was to stop him from flying over palace walls or fortress ramparts?

In the days that followed, Hezarfen found himself summoned to the palace. The Sultan, while outwardly congratulatory, made it clear that such experiments were not to continue. The official stance was that Hezarfen's talents could be better used elsewhere, perhaps in service to the military or the court.

Hezarfen understood the unspoken warning. His dream of further flights, of perfecting his design and perhaps even teaching others, was abruptly grounded. He was given a position in Algeria, ostensibly as a reward, but in reality, a form of exile.

As he prepared to leave Istanbul, Hezarfen took one last look at the city from the top of Galata Tower. The view that had once filled him with excitement now brought a bittersweet pang. He had tasted freedom in its purest form, had glimpsed a future of limitless possibility. And now, that future was being taken from him.

Yet even as he sailed away from the city he loved, Hezarfen knew that his flight had changed something fundamental. He had proven that the impossible was possible, that the dreams of centuries could be made real through determination and ingenuity.

. . .

In the years that followed, Hezarfen's story took on a life of its own. It became a legend, passed down through generations, growing and changing with each retelling. Some versions claimed he'd flown much further than Üsküdar, others that he'd performed multiple flights before being stopped. The truth became intertwined with fantasy, but the core of the story remained: a man had flown.

Centuries later, as the first airplanes took to the skies, some remembered the tale of Hezarfen Ahmed Çelebi. His flight, brief though it was, had been a spark - a moment when the boundary between the possible and impossible had blurred, opening minds to new horizons.

Today, visitors to Istanbul can still climb Galata Tower and look out over the Bosphorus to Üsküdar. The view hasn't changed much since Hezarfen's time, but the skies are different. Airplanes crisscross overhead, carrying passengers on journeys that would have seemed like pure fantasy in the 17th century.

And yet, there's something about Hezarfen's story that continues to captivate. Perhaps it's the romance of that first flight, the image of a lone man soaring over the city on homemade wings. Or perhaps it's the reminder that progress often comes at a cost, that visionaries are not always appreciated in their own time.

Whatever the reason, the legend of Hezarfen Ahmed Çelebi remains a beloved part of Istanbul's lore. It speaks to the city's long history of innovation and to the universal human desire to break free from earthly constraints. In a world where air travel has become commonplace, Hezarfen's brief flight across the

Bosphorus still has the power to inspire wonder and spark the imagination.

For in that moment, suspended between Europe and Asia, between the past and the future, Hezarfen embodied the spirit of discovery that has driven human progress for millennia. His flight may have been brief, but its impact echoes through time, a testament to the power of dreams and the indomitable human spirit.

3

THE MYSTERY OF THE BASILICA CISTERN'S MEDUSA HEADS

Beneath the streets of Istanbul lies a hidden world of shadows and secrets. The Basilica Cistern, a vast underground chamber built in the 6th century, holds within its depths a mystery that has puzzled visitors and scholars for centuries: the enigmatic Medusa heads.

As you descend the worn stone steps into the cistern, the air grows cool and damp. The sound of dripping water echoes off ancient brick walls, and the flickering light of strategically placed lamps creates an otherworldly atmosphere. Rows upon rows of marble columns stretch into the gloom, their reflections shimmering in the shallow pool that covers the floor.

But it's not the sheer scale of this subterranean marvel that captures the imagination of most visitors. It's what lies at the far corner of the chamber, supporting two of the massive columns: a pair of colossal Medusa heads, their stone faces frozen in eternal expressions of defiance.

What makes these sculptures truly perplexing is their positioning. One head lies on its side, while the other is inverted, staring at the ceiling with unseeing eyes. It's a deliberate arrangement that seems to defy logic and convention, sparking countless theories and legends over the years.

The Medusa heads themselves are masterpieces of ancient sculpture, believed to date back to the 2nd or 3rd century AD. They depict the Gorgon of Greek mythology, a fearsome creature with snakes for hair, whose gaze could turn mortals to stone. In classical art, Medusa was often used as a protective symbol, her terrifying visage meant to ward off evil spirits and enemies.

But why would such powerful talismans be placed in the foundations of a water storage facility? And why position them in such an unusual manner?

Some historians suggest a practical explanation. The heads may have been repurposed from an earlier building, used as convenient supports for the columns without regard for their artistic or symbolic value. In the Byzantine era, it wasn't uncommon for builders to incorporate older architectural elements into new structures, a practice known as spoliation.

This theory, however, doesn't fully account for the deliberate positioning of the heads. If they were merely being used as building materials, why take the time to arrange them so precisely?

Others believe the unusual placement was a deliberate act of Christian iconoclasm. By the time the cistern was built, the Roman Empire had embraced Christianity, and pagan symbols like Medusa were often defaced or repositioned as a way of neutralizing their power. Turning the heads sideways and upside-down could have been a symbolic victory of the new faith over the old gods.

But this explanation, too, has its flaws. If the goal was to disrespect or negate the pagan imagery, why use the Medusa heads at all? Surely there were other, less symbolically charged stones that could have served as column bases.

A more intriguing theory draws on the esoteric beliefs that permeated Byzantine society. Some scholars argue that the positioning of the heads was part of a complex magical or religious ritual, designed to harness Medusa's protective power while also rendering her gaze harmless.

In this interpretation, the sideways head represents the negation of evil coming from one direction, while the inverted head symbolizes evil being sent back to the underworld. Together, they create a powerful ward, protecting the water supply - a crucial resource in a city frequently under siege - from both physical and spiritual contamination.

This theory gains some credence when we consider the importance of water in Byzantine religious and magical practices. Blessed water was believed to have healing and purifying properties, and the Basilica Cistern, with its forest of columns and mysterious depths, may have been seen as more than just a practical storage facility.

Adding to the mystery is the fact that these are not the only unusual features of the cistern. Among the 336 columns that support the vaulted ceiling, two stand out: their bases are carved with the likeness of Medusa's mythological sister, the Gorgon Stheno. Unlike the more famous heads, these carvings are positioned normally, facing outward as if guarding the watery realm.

The presence of these additional Gorgon images suggests that the use of mythological figures in the cistern was not random, but part of a larger symbolic or decorative scheme. But what exactly that scheme was remains a matter of speculation.

Over the centuries, the mystery of the Medusa heads has given rise to numerous legends and folktales. One popular story claims that the heads were placed there to protect the cistern from evil spirits that might contaminate the water. Another suggests that looking directly at the faces would turn the viewer to stone, hence their unusual positioning.

. . .

Some tales go even further, weaving the Medusa heads into elaborate narratives of secret societies and hidden treasures. There are those who believe that the cistern holds clues to long-lost Byzantine riches, with the Medusa heads serving as markers or guardians of this mythical hoard.

While these stories may be more fiction than fact, they speak to the enduring power of the Medusa heads to captivate the imagination. In a city layered with history, where the ancient and the modern exist side by side, these enigmatic sculptures represent a tangible link to a distant past shrouded in mystery.

Today, the Basilica Cistern is a popular tourist attraction, drawing visitors from around the world who come to marvel at its atmospheric beauty and ponder the riddle of the Medusa heads. As you walk the raised platforms that crisscross the cistern, the soft lighting and haunting music create an almost theatrical experience, encouraging visitors to lose themselves in the mysteries of the past.

The heads themselves, worn by time and the constant drip of water, retain a powerful presence. Their unseeing eyes seem to follow you as you move through the chamber, and it's easy to imagine them coming to life in the flickering shadows.

But perhaps the true value of the Medusa heads lies not in solving their mystery, but in the questions they continue to provoke. They remind us that history is not a fixed narrative, but a constantly evolving dialogue between the past and the present. Each generation brings new perspectives, new theories, and new ways of understanding the relics left behind by our ancestors.

. . .

In this sense, the Medusa heads of the Basilica Cistern are more than just ancient sculptures or architectural curiosities. They are a challenge to our imagination, an invitation to look beyond the surface and consider the countless stories and possibilities that lie hidden in the layers of history beneath our feet.

As you ascend the steps back to the busy streets of modern Istanbul, the image of those stone faces lingers in your mind. In a city where the past is always present, where empires have risen and fallen and risen again, the mystery of the Medusa heads stands as a testament to the enduring power of myth and the human desire to make sense of the inexplicable.

And so the debate continues, each new visitor forming their own theories, each generation adding its own layer to the legend. The Medusa heads keep their silent vigil, their secrets safe for now, waiting for the day when their true purpose might finally be revealed.

4

SÜMBÜL EFENDI

In the winding streets of 16th century Istanbul, where the scent of spices mingled with the call to prayer, there lived a man known as Sümbül Efendi. His name, meaning "hyacinth" in Turkish, was fitting for one whose presence seemed to bring a spiritual fragrance wherever he went. Sümbül Efendi was a Sufi sheikh, a mystic whose teachings and reputed miracles had earned him a devoted following among both the common people and the Ottoman elite.

. . .

Born Yusuf Sinani, he had come to Istanbul from Egypt as a young man, drawn by the city's reputation as a center of Islamic learning. Under the tutelage of renowned scholars, he had delved deep into the esoteric teachings of Sufism, seeking a direct, personal experience of the divine. As his wisdom and reputation grew, so did the number of his disciples, and soon he was given the honorific title of "Efendi" - master.

But it wasn't just his teachings that drew people to Sümbül Efendi. Stories of his miraculous deeds spread through the city like wildfire, whispered in marketplaces and recounted in the quiet corners of mosques. Some said he could heal the sick with a touch, others that he could read the hearts of men as easily as others read books. But of all the tales told about Sümbül Efendi, none captured the imagination quite like the story of the tavern that became a mosque.

In those days, Istanbul was a city of contrasts. Despite the official prohibition of alcohol in Islamic law, taverns could be found tucked away in certain neighborhoods, catering to sailors, soldiers, and others who sought escape in the bottom of a cup. One such establishment stood in the shadow of the great mosques, a constant source of tension between the pious and the profane.

The tavern was known for its raucous atmosphere and potent wine. Night after night, it drew in those who wished to forget their troubles or celebrate their fortunes, its windows glowing with lamplight long after the rest of the city had gone to sleep. The sound of laughter and drunken songs often drowned out the final call to prayer, much to the dismay of the neighborhood's more devout residents.

·   ·   ·

Many had tried to shut the tavern down or convince its patrons to change their ways, but to no avail. The owner was well-connected, and his customers were not interested in sermons or threats. It seemed the tavern would remain a thorn in the side of the faithful indefinitely.

Enter Sümbül Efendi. One evening, as the sun was setting and the tavern was just beginning to fill with its usual crowd, the Sufi saint appeared at its door. He was an imposing figure, with a long beard and piercing eyes that seemed to look right through you. The patrons fell silent as he entered, some out of respect, others out of curiosity, and a few out of fear.

Without a word, Sümbül Efendi made his way to the center of the room. There, he closed his eyes and began to turn slowly, his robes swirling around him. As he turned, he began to chant, his voice low at first but gradually growing in volume and intensity.

The tavern-goers watched in amazement as Sümbül Efendi spun faster and faster, his chant becoming a mesmerizing melody that seemed to fill not just the room, but their very souls. Some later swore they saw a soft light emanating from the Sufi's body, while others claimed the very air seemed to shimmer with spiritual energy.

As the night wore on, something extraordinary began to happen. One by one, the patrons found themselves setting down their cups, drawn into the rhythm of Sümbül Efendi's dance. The raucous laughter faded, replaced by a profound silence broken only by the sound of the saint's voice.

· · ·

Hours passed, though to those present it felt like both an eternity and an instant. As the first light of dawn began to creep through the windows, Sümbül Efendi finally came to a stop. He opened his eyes and looked around the room, a gentle smile on his face.

The tavern-goers blinked, as if waking from a dream. But as they looked around, they realized that it was no dream. The tavern had been transformed. Where once there had been tables sticky with spilled wine, there were now prayer rugs. The bar had become a mihrab, indicating the direction of Mecca. Even the air seemed different, the scent of incense replacing the stale odor of alcohol.

But the physical transformation was nothing compared to the change in the hearts of those present. Men who had entered the tavern as hardened drinkers now felt a burning desire to prostrate themselves in prayer. The owner, who had stubbornly resisted all previous attempts to close his business, now declared his intention to donate the building as a mosque.

As word of the miracle spread, people flocked to the new mosque to see for themselves. Many were skeptical at first, unable to believe that such a dramatic transformation could happen overnight. But as they listened to the testimony of those who had been present, and as they felt the unmistakable atmosphere of sanctity that now pervaded the building, even the doubters began to believe.

Sümbül Efendi himself said little about the event, preferring to let his actions speak for themselves. When pressed, he would only say that it was not he who had performed the miracle, but rather the divine power working through him. His humility only served to increase the awe in which he was held by the people of Istanbul.

The story of the tavern-turned-mosque quickly became a favorite tale among the city's storytellers. In the coffee houses and market-places, people would gather to hear it recounted, each telling adding new details and embellishments. Some versions claimed that the wine in the tavern's cellar had turned to rosewater, while others insisted that the transformation had been accompanied by a host of angels visible only to the pure of heart.

For Sümbül Efendi, the event marked a turning point. Already respected as a spiritual leader, he now found himself elevated to the status of a living saint. People came from far and wide to seek his blessing or to ask for his intercession in their prayers. The Ottoman Sultan himself is said to have consulted Sümbül Efendi on matters of state, valuing the Sufi's wisdom and reputed ability to see beyond the veil of ordinary reality.

But with this increased fame came increased scrutiny. Not everyone was comfortable with the idea of a man who could perform such miraculous deeds. Some of the more conservative religious scholars viewed Sümbül Efendi's mystical practices with suspicion, arguing that they strayed too far from orthodox Islam. Others, particularly those with vested interests in the city's less savory entertainments, saw him as a threat to their livelihoods.

Sümbül Efendi met these challenges with the same equanimity he brought to all aspects of his life. He continued to teach and to practice his mystical devotions, neither seeking confrontation nor backing down from it when it came to him. His followers, fiercely loyal, defended him passionately against any accusations of impropriety or heresy.

As the years passed, the story of the tavern's transformation took on a life of its own. It became more than just a tale of a miraculous event; it became a parable about the power of faith to transform even the most unlikely hearts. For many in Istanbul, the mosque stood as a physical reminder that change was always possible, that no one was beyond redemption.

Sümbül Efendi lived to a ripe old age, continuing to teach and inspire until his last days. When he finally passed away, the city mourned as one. He was buried near the mosque that bore his name, the very building that had once been a tavern. His tomb became a place of pilgrimage, visited by those seeking blessings or hoping to absorb some of the spiritual power that had radiated from him in life.

Today, centuries later, the Sümbül Efendi Mosque still stands in Istanbul, a testament to the enduring power of the saint's legend. While modern historians may debate the literal truth of the tavern's overnight transformation, the story continues to captivate those who hear it. It speaks to a deep human desire for transformation, for the possibility of radical change in the blink of an eye.

Visitors to the mosque often pause to reflect on the strange twists of fate that led to its creation. Some claim to feel a special energy within its walls, a lingering trace of the spiritual power that Sümbül Efendi wielded. Others simply appreciate the beauty of its architecture and the peaceful atmosphere that pervades it.

· · ·

For the people of Istanbul, the story of Sümbül Efendi and the tavern that became a mosque is more than just a colorful piece of local folklore. It's a reminder of their city's rich spiritual heritage, a heritage that encompasses not just the grand mosques and palaces, but also the small miracles that happen in unexpected places. In a city where the past and present coexist in every street and alleyway, Sümbül Efendi's legend continues to inspire, reminding all who hear it that transformation - be it of a building, a person, or a society - is always possible for those with faith and an open heart.

5

___

ALI USTA'S GOLDEN HANDS

In the busy workshops of 16th century Istanbul, one name stood out among the city's many artisans: Ali Usta. Known for his unparalleled skill in metalwork, Ali could transform raw materials into objects of breathtaking beauty. His creations graced the palaces of sultans and the homes of wealthy merchants, each piece a testament to his mastery of his craft.

. . .

Ali had come from humble beginnings, the son of a blacksmith in a small Anatolian village. From a young age, he had shown an extraordinary aptitude for working with metal. Where other apprentices struggled to shape the simplest objects, Ali's hands seemed to possess an almost magical ability to coax beauty from the most unyielding materials.

As word of his talent spread, Ali was eventually summoned to Istanbul, the heart of the Ottoman Empire. There, he found himself in a world of opportunity and competition. The city was a melting pot of cultures and artistic traditions, with craftsmen from across the empire vying for the patronage of the wealthy and powerful.

But Ali was undaunted by the challenge. He threw himself into his work with a passion that bordered on obsession, pushing the boundaries of his craft in ways that left his peers in awe. His workshop became a place of wonder, where ordinary metals were transformed into extraordinary works of art.

Ali's creations were unlike anything seen before in Istanbul. He crafted intricate jewelry that seemed to capture the very essence of light, ornate water pitchers that made the act of pouring a work of performance art, and ceremonial swords so perfectly balanced they felt like extensions of the wielder's arm. But it was his lanterns that truly set him apart.

These were no ordinary light sources. Ali's lanterns were masterpieces of metalwork and design, their delicate filigree patterns casting enchanting shadows that danced and shifted with the flame within. Each one was unique, a reflection of the personality and desires of its owner. It was said that to possess one of Ali's lanterns was to hold a piece of captured starlight.

As Ali's fame grew, so did the demand for his work. Nobles and merchants competed for his attention, offering ever-increasing sums for his creations. Even the Sultan himself took notice, commissioning Ali to create a series of lanterns for the imperial palace.

For most artisans, such recognition would have been the pinnacle of their career. But Ali was driven by something beyond mere ambition or desire for wealth. He saw his work as a form of devotion, a way of revealing the hidden beauty of the world through his craft. Each piece he created was a prayer made manifest in metal and gems.

It was this spiritual dimension to his work that set Ali apart from his contemporaries. While others were content to repeat familiar patterns and techniques, Ali constantly sought new ways to express the inexpressible through his art. He studied not just metalworking, but mathematics, astronomy, and even Sufi mysticism, incorporating elements of sacred geometry and cosmic symbolism into his designs.

This blend of technical mastery and spiritual insight resulted in works of such profound beauty that they moved even the most hardened hearts. There were stories of hardened warriors weeping at the sight of Ali's creations, and of rival artisans laying down their tools in humble acknowledgment of his superiority.

. . .

But as Ali's star rose ever higher, dark clouds began to gather on the horizon. His success had bred jealousy among some of his fellow craftsmen, who saw their own patronage dwindling as more and more customers flocked to Ali's workshop. Whispers began to circulate, suggesting that Ali's uncanny skill must be the result of some dark bargain or forbidden magic.

These rumors eventually reached the ears of the Sultan, a man known for his mercurial temper and suspicious nature. The Sultan had always been sensitive to perceived threats to his authority, and the idea that a mere craftsman could wield such power over people's hearts and minds began to gnaw at him.

One fateful day, the Sultan summoned Ali to the palace. The artisan arrived bearing his latest creation, a lantern of surpassing beauty commissioned for the Sultan's favorite concubine. But as Ali unveiled the piece, he found not wonder in the Sultan's eyes, but cold fury.

Driven by jealousy and fear, the Sultan accused Ali of sorcery, claiming that no mortal hands could create such beauty without the aid of dark powers. In a fit of rage, he ordered that Ali's hands, the source of his supposed magic, be cut off.

The sentence was carried out immediately, there in the opulent halls of the palace. Ali's anguished cries echoed through the corridors as his hands, the instruments of his art and the extension of his very soul, were severed from his body.

For many, this would have been the end of the story. A craftsman without hands is like a bird without wings, his art forever silenced. But Ali's story was far from over.

In the days that followed his mutilation, Ali sank into a deep despair. He retreated to his home, refusing to see anyone, even his closest friends and apprentices. Those who caught glimpses of him reported that he spent hours staring at the stumps of his wrists, as if willing his hands to regrow through sheer force of will.

But as the weeks passed, something began to change within Ali. The initial shock and despair gave way to a smoldering determination. If he could no longer create with his hands, he would find another way. His art, he realized, came not from his hands alone, but from his mind, his heart, and his indomitable spirit.

And so, in secret, Ali began to teach himself to work with his feet. It was an agonizing process, filled with frustration and setbacks. Many times he was tempted to give up, to accept that his life as an artisan was over. But each time he came close to surrendering, he would remember the joy of creation, the feeling of shaping beauty from raw materials, and he would push on.

Months passed, and slowly, painstakingly, Ali began to regain his skill. His feet learned to grasp tools with the same dexterity his hands had once possessed. He developed new techniques, new ways of manipulating metal that compensated for his lost hands. And as he worked, he found that his ordeal had given him a new perspective, a deeper understanding of the interplay between limitation and creativity.

· · ·

Finally, after more than a year of secret toil, Ali emerged from his seclusion. He announced that he was ready to work again, and that he would create a piece unlike any he had made before.

The news spread through Istanbul like wildfire. Many were skeptical, unable to believe that a man without hands could still practice such a demanding craft. Others, remembering Ali's former greatness, dared to hope for a miracle.

When the day came for Ali to unveil his new creation, it seemed all of Istanbul had gathered to witness the event. The crowd waited with bated breath as Ali, his arms ending in scarred stumps, stood before a veiled object.

With a nod, Ali signaled for the veil to be lifted, and a collective gasp rose from the crowd. There, gleaming in the sunlight, stood a lantern of such exquisite beauty that it brought tears to the eyes of all who beheld it.

The lantern was a masterpiece, its intricate designs telling the story of Ali's journey from despair to triumph. Delicate filigree work depicted hands reaching for the stars, while the play of light and shadow seemed to symbolize the constant struggle between darkness and illumination.

But it was more than just a beautiful object. Those who looked upon it felt their spirits lifted, their own struggles put into perspective. It was as if Ali had poured not just his skill, but his very soul into the piece, creating something that transcended mere craftsmanship to become a testament to the resilience of the human spirit.

·   ·   ·

The Sultan, hearing of Ali's triumphant return, was torn between admiration and shame. In a gesture of reconciliation, he offered Ali a position as the chief royal artisan, with wealth and honors beyond measure. But Ali, who had learned that true art comes from freedom rather than patronage, politely declined.

Instead, Ali chose to open a school, passing on his hard-won knowledge to a new generation of craftsmen. He taught them not just the techniques of metalwork, but the deeper lessons he had learned: that true mastery comes from within, that limitations can be the seeds of innovation, and that the greatest art speaks not just to the eyes, but to the heart and soul.

In the years that followed, Ali's fame only grew. His new works, created with his feet, were even more sought after than his earlier pieces. People came from across the empire and beyond to study with him or to commission works. And though he never regained the use of his hands, Ali found that he had gained something far more valuable: a deeper understanding of his art and of himself.

Today, few of Ali's original works survive, victims of time and the vicissitudes of history. But his legacy lives on in the techniques he developed, in the school he founded, and in the enduring legend of the craftsman who turned tragedy into triumph. In the workshops of Istanbul, artisans still speak of Ali Usta, the man whose golden hands were in his heart, not his limbs, and whose greatest creation was not an object, but an example of the indomitable nature of the human spirit.

THE LAUGHING TOMBSTONE

In the sprawling Eyüp Cemetery, where centuries of Istanbul's departed rest beneath towering cypress trees, there's a tombstone that stands out from the rest. It's not its shape or size that draws attention, but the strange sound that some claim to hear emanating from it on quiet nights - the faint echo of laughter.

. . .

The story of the Laughing Tombstone dates back to the late Ottoman period, in the waning years of the 19th century. It centers around a man named Hüseyin, known throughout his neighborhood for his jovial nature and boisterous laugh. Hüseyin wasn't a man of great importance or wealth, but his ability to find humor in any situation made him a beloved figure in his community.

Hüseyin worked as a scribe in one of the many government offices that kept the sprawling Ottoman bureaucracy functioning. It was a job that many would have found tedious, but Hüseyin approached it with a perpetual twinkle in his eye. He found amusement in the absurdities of official language, in the quirks of his colleagues, and in the daily parade of humanity that passed through his office.

But it was after work that Hüseyin truly came alive. He was a fixture in the local coffeehouses, where he would regale his friends with humorous tales and witty observations. His laugh was unmistakable - a deep, belly-shaking guffaw that would start softly and build to a crescendo, often causing those around him to join in even if they hadn't heard the joke.

Hüseyin's wife, Fatma, would often chide him for his excessive mirth. "One day that laugh will be the death of you," she'd say, half-jokingly. Hüseyin would respond with a wink and another chuckle, assuring her that there were far worse ways to go.

As it turned out, Fatma's playful warning would prove prophetic. On a warm summer evening, Hüseyin was at his favorite coffeehouse, engaged in a lively discussion with friends. Someone - the exact identity has been lost to time - told a joke so hilarious that it sent Hüseyin into paroxysms of laughter.

·   ·   ·

He laughed and laughed, his face turning red, tears streaming down his cheeks. His friends, at first laughing along, began to grow concerned as Hüseyin showed no signs of stopping. His laughter took on a desperate quality, becoming more of a wheeze as he struggled to catch his breath.

Before anyone could intervene, Hüseyin collapsed, his last breath escaping as a final chuckle. The official cause was listed as a heart attack, but everyone knew that Hüseyin had, quite literally, laughed himself to death.

The neighborhood was stunned by the loss of their resident merrymaker. Hüseyin's funeral was a somber affair, despite the deceased's lifelong efforts to keep sorrow at bay. He was laid to rest in the Eyüp Cemetery, his tombstone a simple marble affair with the standard inscriptions - name, dates, a brief prayer.

It was about a week after the funeral that the first strange reports began to circulate. A night watchman, making his rounds through the cemetery, claimed to have heard the sound of laughter coming from the direction of Hüseyin's grave. At first, he dismissed it as his imagination or perhaps the wind playing tricks. But as he drew closer to the tombstone, the sound became unmistakable - a faint but distinct chuckle that seemed to emanate from the very ground.

The watchman fled, convinced he had encountered a spirit. When he reported the incident to his superiors, he was met with skepticism and gentle mockery. But over the following weeks, others began to report similar experiences. Visitors to nearby graves would hurry past Hüseyin's tombstone, unnerved by the muffled sounds of mirth that seemed to follow them.

. . .

As word spread, the Laughing Tombstone became something of a local legend. Some saw it as a heartwarming sign that Hüseyin's jovial spirit lived on. Others viewed it with suspicion, worried that it might be a manifestation of a restless soul or some sort of supernatural mischief.

Theories abounded as to the cause of the phenomenon. Some suggested that Hüseyin's widow, unable to bear her grief, had installed some sort of mechanical device in the tombstone to keep her husband's memory alive. Others proposed more mystical explanations, claiming that Hüseyin's life force had been so strongly tied to laughter that it continued to express itself even after death.

The more scientifically minded put forth the idea that the tombstone's material or shape might be causing it to amplify natural sounds in an unusual way, creating an auditory illusion of laughter. But no matter how many explanations were offered, none seemed to fully account for the experiences reported by so many different people.

As the years passed, the legend of the Laughing Tombstone grew. It became a rite of passage for local youths to spend a night near Hüseyin's grave, waiting to hear the spectral chuckle. Most returned disappointed, hearing nothing but the rustle of leaves and the distant sounds of the city. But every so often, someone would come back wide-eyed, swearing they had heard the unmistakable sound of Hüseyin's laughter.

The tombstone became a draw for tourists as well, particularly those interested in the supernatural. Ghost hunters and paranormal investigators would set up equipment near the grave, hoping to capture evidence of the otherworldly laughter. Their results were inconclusive, but the stories they brought back only added to the tombstone's mystique.

For the caretakers of Eyüp Cemetery, the Laughing Tombstone presented a unique challenge. On one hand, the increased foot traffic and attention were concerning in a place meant for quiet reflection and respect for the dead. On the other hand, the legend brought a certain vibrancy to the cemetery, reminding visitors that death need not always be approached with unrelenting solemnity.

The story took on new dimensions as it was passed down through generations. Some claimed that hearing the laughter was a sign of good fortune, that Hüseyin's spirit was blessing those who visited with joy and prosperity. Others warned that dwelling too long near the tombstone could drive one to madness, overcome by an uncontrollable urge to laugh.

Local artists found inspiration in the tale. Poets wrote verses about the man whose laughter defied death. Painters created works depicting Hüseyin's spirit rising from the grave in peals of laughter. One sculptor even proposed creating a special monument to replace the original tombstone, designed to capture and amplify the sound of the wind in a way that mimicked laughter, but the idea was ultimately rejected as too irreverent.

The legend also sparked philosophical discussions about the nature of joy and the human spirit. Some saw in Hüseyin's story a powerful metaphor for living life to the fullest, finding humor and happiness even in the face of mortality. Others viewed it as a cautionary tale about the dangers of excess, even in something as seemingly positive as laughter.

．　．　．

For the descendants of Hüseyin, the Laughing Tombstone was a source of both pride and occasional embarrassment. They were touched that their ancestor was remembered so fondly, but sometimes grew weary of the constant stream of curiosity seekers and ghost hunters. Some embraced the legend, happily sharing stories of their famous forebear with anyone who asked. Others preferred to distance themselves from what they saw as a silly superstition.

As Istanbul grew and changed around it, the Eyüp Cemetery remained a place of peace and remembrance, with the Laughing Tombstone adding its own unique note to the atmosphere. On quiet nights, when the city's usual clamor dies down and the cemetery is shrouded in mist, some swear they can still hear the faint sound of Hüseyin's laughter carried on the breeze.

Whether the Laughing Tombstone is truly haunted by a merry spirit, is simply the product of overactive imaginations, or falls somewhere in between, its legend has become an integral part of Istanbul's rich tapestry of stories. It serves as a reminder that even in death, the essence of a person - their joy, their passion, their laughter - can live on, echoing through time and touching the lives of generations to come.

For those who visit Eyüp Cemetery today, whether out of respect for the dead, curiosity about the supernatural, or simply to enjoy a moment of quiet in the bustling city, the Laughing Tombstone offers a unique perspective on life, death, and the power of a good laugh. It stands as a testament to the idea that our legacies are not always what we expect them to be, and that sometimes, the most profound impact we can have on the world is simply to bring a little more joy into it.

. . .

As the sun sets over Istanbul and the shadows lengthen in Eyüp Cemetery, one can almost imagine Hüseyin's spirit watching over his final resting place, amused by the attention his tombstone continues to attract. And perhaps, if you listen closely on a still night, you might just hear a faint chuckle carried on the wind - a final joke shared by a man who found humor in life, death, and everything in between.

7

THE MAN WHO SOLD THE GALATA BRIDGE

The Galata Bridge, spanning the Golden Horn and connecting the old city of Istanbul to the more modern Beyoğlu district, has long been a symbol of the city's unique position bridging East and West. But in the 1950s, this iconic structure became the centerpiece of one of the most audacious and legendary con jobs in Istanbul's history, courtesy of a smooth-talking trickster named Sülün Osman.

. . .

Osman, whose nickname "Sülün" means "pheasant" in Turkish, was born into poverty in the early 1920s. Growing up on the rough streets of Istanbul, he learned early on that wit and charm could be powerful tools for survival. By his early thirties, Osman had developed a reputation as a skilled con artist, but it was his scheme to "sell" the Galata Bridge that would cement his place in the annals of Istanbul's folklore.

The 1950s were a time of rapid change and urbanization in Turkey. Istanbul, always a magnet for those seeking opportunity, saw an influx of rural migrants hoping to make their fortunes in the big city. It was these newcomers, often naive about the ways of urban life, who became the primary targets of Osman's audacious scam.

Osman's modus operandi was as simple as it was brazen. Dressed impeccably in a tailored suit and fedora, he would patrol the areas around the Galata Bridge, keeping an eye out for potential marks. His keen eye could spot a newcomer to the city from a mile away - the wide-eyed look, the provincial clothing, the air of someone trying to find their footing in an overwhelming urban landscape.

Once he identified a target, Osman would strike up a conversation, his charisma and friendly demeanor quickly putting the newcomer at ease. He would spin tales of the city's wonders and opportunities, gradually steering the conversation towards the Galata Bridge itself. With a conspiratorial air, he would reveal that he was actually a government official tasked with selling the bridge to private investors.

The sale, Osman would explain, was part of a new initiative to modernize the city's infrastructure. The buyer would have the right to collect tolls from pedestrians and vehicles crossing the bridge, potentially earning a fortune. Of course, such a lucrative opportunity wasn't available to just anyone - but Osman would hint that he might be willing to bend the rules for the right person.

To lend credibility to his claim, Osman would produce official-looking documents, complete with government seals and signatures. These were, in fact, masterfully forged papers that he had crafted himself or obtained through his network of underworld connections. He would also point out the toll booths on the bridge (which were actually used for collecting a real municipal fee) as proof of the potential income.

The coup de grâce of Osman's performance was often a prearranged phone call. At a crucial moment in his sales pitch, a confederate would call him on a nearby payphone, posing as a wealthy businessman interested in buying the bridge. Osman would make a show of reluctantly turning down the offer, telling his mark that he preferred to sell to a "real Anatolian" rather than some rich city slicker.

This combination of apparent insider knowledge, official documentation, and the fear of missing out on a golden opportunity proved irresistible to many of Osman's targets. Farmers who had come to the city with their life savings, hoping to start a new life, would eagerly hand over their money for a chance to own a piece of Istanbul's history and secure a steady income.

Of course, the victims would soon realize they had been duped. Some would return to the bridge, looking in vain for Osman or trying to collect tolls themselves, only to be met with confusion and ridicule from passersby and authorities. By then, Sülün Osman would be long gone, already setting up his next big score.

The Galata Bridge wasn't Osman's only target. He was equally adept at "selling" other Istanbul landmarks, including the Sultanahmet Mosque and even the Dolmabahçe Palace. Each sale was tailored to the specific mark, with Osman adapting his story and approach based on what he thought would be most convincing.

As Osman's successes mounted, so did his reputation. He became something of a local legend, with stories of his exploits spreading through the city's coffeehouses and markets. Some viewed him as a menace, preying on the dreams of innocent people. Others, however, saw him as a folk hero of sorts - a working-class boy who used his wits to outsmart the system and take advantage of the greedy and gullible.

The authorities, naturally, took a dim view of Osman's activities. Police launched numerous attempts to catch him in the act, but Osman's street smarts and network of informants always seemed to keep him one step ahead of the law. He was arrested several times throughout the 1950s, but lack of evidence or his own cunning always saw him back on the streets before long.

Osman's most famous escape came after he was finally caught red-handed trying to sell the Galata Bridge. Brought before a judge, he managed to convince the court that he was mentally unstable and not responsible for his actions. He was committed to a psychiatric hospital instead of prison - only to smooth-talk his way out of the institution just a few days later.

. . .

As the decade wore on and Istanbul continued to modernize, Osman found it increasingly difficult to find easy marks for his bridge-selling scheme. The city's newcomers were becoming more savvy, and increased media coverage of his exploits meant that more people were aware of his tactics.

Undeterred, Osman adapted his cons to the changing times. He moved on to more sophisticated schemes, including real estate fraud and investment scams. But none of these later cons ever captured the public imagination quite like his audacious "sales" of the Galata Bridge.

By the 1960s, Sülün Osman's reign as Istanbul's king of cons was coming to an end. Increased police pressure and the changing nature of the city meant that his old tricks were no longer as effective. He was arrested several more times and spent periods in prison, though his charm and wit often earned him preferential treatment even behind bars.

In his later years, Osman became a colorful figure in Istanbul's social scene. No longer actively conning people, he instead regaled audiences in taverns and cafes with tales of his exploits. He even became something of a media personality, giving interviews and appearing on television shows to share his stories and insights into the art of the con.

Osman's legacy in Istanbul's popular culture is a complex one. While his actions were undoubtedly criminal and caused real harm to his victims, many Istanbul residents retain a certain fondness for the Galata Bridge swindler. His exploits have been the subject of books, films, and even stage plays, often portrayed with a mix of condemnation and grudging admiration.

. . .

For many, Sülün Osman represents a particular moment in Istanbul's history - a time when the city was rapidly changing, when fortunes could be made or lost in an instant, and when a quick wit and silver tongue could take you far. His story is seen as a quintessentially Istanbul tale, embodying the city's reputation as a place of both opportunity and danger, where nothing is quite as it seems.

Today, tourists crossing the Galata Bridge might hear tour guides recount the tale of Sülün Osman and his infamous scam. The story serves as both a colorful anecdote and a gentle warning to be wary of modern-day tricksters who might prey on visitors.

The bridge itself, rebuilt several times since Osman's heyday, remains a vital part of Istanbul's landscape. Fishermen line its rails, cafes bustle beneath its span, and thousands cross it daily, most unaware that they're walking across a piece of con artist history.

Sülün Osman's tale, like the city of Istanbul itself, is one of contrasts and contradictions. It's a story of crime and cunning, of ambition and audacity, of a man who saw the Galata Bridge not as a means of connection, but as an opportunity for deception. Yet it's also a story that captures something essential about Istanbul - its energy, its complexity, and its endless capacity to produce legends.

As the sun sets over the Golden Horn and the lights of the Galata Bridge twinkle to life, one can almost imagine Sülün Osman still patrolling its length, fedora tilted rakishly, eyes peeled for the next big score. His physical presence may be gone, but his spirit lives on in the bridge he so famously "sold," a permanent part of Istanbul's rich tapestry of myths and memories.

8

THE BRIDGE OF SPIES

The Bosphorus Bridge, spanning the narrow strait that divides Europe and Asia, has long been more than just a feat of engineering. During the Cold War, this iconic structure earned a far more intriguing moniker: the Bridge of Spies. As the sun set and Istanbul's lights flickered to life, the bridge transformed into a stage for high-stakes espionage, where agents from East and West played out their dangerous games.

. . .

Istanbul's unique geography made it an ideal setting for covert operations. Straddling two continents, the city was a natural crossroads for international intrigue. Its bustling bazaars, crowded streets, and labyrinthine alleys provided perfect cover for clandestine meetings and drop-offs. But it was the Bosphorus Bridge, completed in 1973, that became the focal point for many of these shadowy encounters.

The bridge's appeal to spies was multifaceted. Its length and constant flow of traffic made surveillance difficult. The pedestrian walkways offered opportunities for seemingly casual encounters. And perhaps most importantly, its location - literally bridging East and West - made it a powerfully symbolic meeting point for operatives from both sides of the Iron Curtain.

One of the most notorious regulars on the Bridge of Spies was a man known only as "The Turk." Neither fully aligned with the KGB nor entirely in the pocket of the CIA, The Turk was a freelance information broker who played both sides with remarkable skill. His services were sought after by intelligence agencies around the world, and the Bosphorus Bridge was his preferred venue for business.

On a chilly November night in 1978, The Turk arranged a meeting on the bridge with a nervous young CIA officer named Jack Reeves. Reeves had been in Istanbul for just three months, still finding his footing in the world of international espionage. The meeting was set for midnight, when traffic on the bridge would be light but not suspiciously so.

. . .

Reeves arrived early, his heart pounding as he tried to look casual while scanning the sparse crowd for his contact. The Turk, true to form, appeared out of nowhere, suddenly falling into step beside the American as if they were old friends out for a stroll.

"Beautiful night," The Turk commented in flawless English, his eyes never leaving the distant horizon. "But I hear storm clouds are gathering in the East."

Reeves recognized the coded phrase and responded with the appropriate counter-sign. With pleasantries out of the way, they got down to business. The Turk had information about Soviet troop movements along the Turkish border - information that could be crucial in the ongoing chess game of Cold War politics.

As they walked, The Turk outlined what he knew, his voice barely above a whisper. Reeves listened intently, trying to commit every detail to memory. Halfway across the bridge, they paused, leaning against the railing as if admiring the view of the Bosphorus below.

In a move practiced countless times, Reeves slipped a thick envelope into The Turk's coat pocket. In return, he felt the slight weight of a microfilm canister being pressed into his palm. The exchange was over in seconds, invisible to any casual observer.

As they prepared to part ways, The Turk gripped Reeves' arm, his face suddenly serious. "Be careful, my young friend," he murmured. "The bridge has eyes, and not all of them are friendly."

· · ·

With that cryptic warning, The Turk melted into the night, leaving Reeves to make his way back to the safety of the U.S. Consulate, the valuable microfilm burning a hole in his pocket.

The Turk's warning was not idle. The Bosphorus Bridge, for all its usefulness as a meeting point, was also a dangerous place for spies. Both the KGB and the CIA maintained surveillance on the structure, each trying to catch the other's agents in the act. Local Turkish intelligence, eager to prove their worth to their NATO allies, also kept a close watch on the comings and goings on the bridge.

One of the most feared operatives working the bridge was a KGB agent known as "The Widow." Her real name was Anya Petrova, but she had earned her nickname through her ruthless efficiency in eliminating enemy agents. The Widow was a master of disguise, equally comfortable posing as a glamorous socialite or a hunched old woman selling flowers to tourists.

In the spring of 1980, The Widow set her sights on a British MI6 agent who had been causing trouble for Soviet operations in Turkey. She arranged a meet on the bridge, posing as a potential defector with valuable information about the KGB's Istanbul network.

The British agent, eager for a big score, fell for the trap. As they met in the middle of the bridge, The Widow's demeanor suddenly changed. Before the MI6 man could react, he felt a sharp prick in his side - a poison-tipped umbrella, a favorite tool of KGB assassins.

· · ·

As the agent crumpled to the ground, The Widow calmly walked away, blending seamlessly into a group of late-night revelers crossing the bridge. By the time anyone realized something was wrong, she was long gone, leaving behind a body and a message: the Bridge of Spies was not a game for amateurs.

But not all encounters on the bridge ended in violence. Sometimes, it served as neutral ground for tense negotiations between rival agencies. In 1982, with tensions between the United States and the Soviet Union at a fever pitch, the bridge became the site of a secret meeting between high-level representatives of the CIA and KGB.

The meeting was arranged through back channels, with both sides agreeing to send only two operatives each. The goal was to establish a direct line of communication to prevent misunderstandings that could escalate into open conflict.

On a fog-shrouded night in late October, four figures met at the bridge's midpoint. No names were exchanged, no pleasantries offered. For three tense hours, they talked, each side probing for weaknesses while trying to project strength. In the end, a tenuous agreement was reached - a hotline of sorts, to be used only in the direst of circumstances.

As dawn broke over Istanbul, the four spies parted ways, each heading back to their respective sides of the divide. The bridge had once again lived up to its reputation as a place where East and West could meet, however briefly and warily.

· · ·

The Bridge of Spies wasn't just a venue for professional intelligence operatives. It also attracted its share of amateur spies and thrill-seekers, drawn by the romance and danger of Cold War espionage. These hobbyist spies, while generally harmless, sometimes complicated matters for the professionals.

One such amateur was Mehmet Yılmaz, a Istanbul University student with a vivid imagination and a penchant for detective novels. Convinced he had uncovered a major international conspiracy, Mehmet began spending his evenings on the bridge, watching for suspicious characters and taking copious notes.

Mehmet's activities did not go unnoticed. Both Turkish intelligence and the CIA flagged him as a person of interest, each suspecting he might be working for the other side. The KGB, always on the lookout for potential recruits, even approached Mehmet, thinking he might be a useful asset.

The situation came to a head one night when Mehmet, in his enthusiasm, accidentally interrupted a genuine exchange between Chinese and East German agents. The resulting chaos nearly led to an international incident, with accusations and counter-accusations flying between various intelligence agencies.

In the end, Mehmet was quietly taken aside by Turkish authorities and strongly encouraged to find a less dangerous hobby. But his brief foray into the world of espionage became something of a legend among Istanbul's student population, inspiring others to keep an eye out for spies on the bridge.

. . .

As the Cold War began to thaw in the late 1980s, the Bridge of Spies gradually lost its central role in the world of international espionage. The fall of the Berlin Wall and the collapse of the Soviet Union changed the global intelligence landscape, and Istanbul's importance as a spy hub diminished.

But the legacy of those tense years lived on. Former spies, now retired, would sometimes return to the bridge, drawn by memories of their cloak-and-dagger days. Local tour guides began incorporating stories of the bridge's espionage history into their narratives, thrilling tourists with tales of midnight meetings and narrowly averted crises.

For the people of Istanbul, the Bridge of Spies became a source of pride - a reminder that their city had played a crucial, if often unseen, role in shaping 20th-century history. The bridge stood as a testament to Istanbul's enduring position as a crossroads of cultures and ideologies, a place where East and West could meet, clash, and sometimes find common ground.

Today, as cars and pedestrians cross the Bosphorus Bridge, few may realize the drama that once unfolded on its span. But for those who know where to look, the ghosts of Cold War spies still linger. In the shadows cast by the bridge's imposing towers, in the quiet corners of its pedestrian walkways, the echoes of whispered secrets and hurried exchanges can almost be heard.

The Bridge of Spies may no longer be the hotbed of espionage it once was, but it remains a powerful symbol of Istanbul's unique place in the world. It stands as a reminder that in this city where continents meet, anything is possible - even the most unlikely of encounters between sworn enemies.

•   •   •

As night falls over the Bosphorus and the bridge lights up against the darkening sky, one can almost imagine the silhouettes of figures meeting in the middle, secrets changing hands, fates being decided. The age of Cold War espionage may be over, but the Bridge of Spies continues to capture the imagination, a enduring testament to a time when Istanbul stood at the very center of a world divided.

9

THE GHOST OF ÇEMBERLITAŞ HAMMAM

The Çemberlitaş Hammam stands as a silent sentinel in the heart of Istanbul, its weathered stone walls bearing witness to centuries of history. Built in 1584 by the renowned Ottoman architect Mimar Sinan, the bathhouse has long been a place of relaxation and rejuvenation for locals and visitors alike. But beneath the steam and behind the marble columns lies a tale that has been whispered for generations - the story of a bride whose life was cut tragically short, and whose spirit, some say, still lingers within the hammam's ancient walls.

The legend begins on a warm summer evening in the late 16th century. The city was alive with celebration as a wealthy merchant's daughter prepared for her wedding day. Her name was Ayşe, and she was known throughout the neighborhood for her beauty and kind heart. The groom was a successful trader, and the match was considered ideal by both families.

As was customary, Ayşe spent the day before her wedding at the Çemberlitaş Hammam, accompanied by her female relatives and friends. The bathhouse echoed with laughter and song as the women performed the traditional bridal bath rituals, cleansing and adorning the young bride-to-be.

Ayşe reveled in the attention, her excitement for the upcoming nuptials evident in her glowing smile and sparkling eyes. As she was led through the various chambers of the hammam, from the warm room to the hot room and finally to the cooling room, she felt a sense of peace and contentment wash over her. The steam seemed to carry away any lingering doubts or fears, leaving her ready to embrace her new life.

As the evening wore on and the other women began to depart, Ayşe lingered behind, savoring the last moments of her maidenhood. She asked for a few minutes alone to offer a private prayer for her future happiness. Her mother, indulgent of her daughter's wishes on this special day, agreed, promising to return shortly to escort her home.

. . .

But fate had other plans for young Ayşe. As she knelt in prayer, a sudden dizziness overcame her. The steam, which had seemed so soothing earlier, now felt oppressive and thick. She tried to call out, but her voice was lost in the cavernous space of the hammam. The world began to spin, and Ayşe collapsed onto the cool marble floor.

When her mother returned, she found Ayşe lifeless, her skin already growing cold despite the warmth of the bathhouse. The joyous atmosphere of the day shattered into wails of grief and disbelief. How could a young woman, on the cusp of her new life, be struck down so suddenly?

The exact cause of Ayşe's death remained a mystery. Some blamed an undetected heart condition, others whispered of poison slipped into her sherbet by a jealous rival. Regardless of the reason, the result was the same - a bride, adorned for her wedding, was carried to her grave instead of the marriage bed.

In the days that followed, the Çemberlitaş Hammam stood empty, its doors closed out of respect for the tragedy that had occurred within. But as life in the bustling city slowly returned to normal, the bathhouse reopened. Yet something had changed. Attendants spoke in hushed tones of strange occurrences - the sound of weeping echoing through empty chambers, the scent of bridal henna lingering in the air when no brides were present.

At first, these incidents were dismissed as the product of overactive imaginations, minds still dwelling on the sad fate of young Ayşe. But as the years passed and the stories persisted, a new legend began to take shape. People said that Ayşe's spirit, unable to accept her untimely death, remained bound to the place where she had spent her last living moments.

The tales of Ayşe's ghost grew more elaborate with each telling. Some claimed to have seen a young woman in bridal attire wandering the halls of the hammam late at night, her henna-stained hands trailing along the walls. Others reported hearing the soft tinkling of bridal jewelry or catching a glimpse of a veiled figure reflected in the pools of water.

One particularly chilling account came from a night watchman who swore he had encountered the spectral bride. He described how he had been making his rounds when he heard the sound of gentle sobbing coming from the main bathing area. Thinking a guest had been accidentally locked in, he went to investigate. There, seated on the edge of the central fountain, he saw a young woman dressed in an ornate wedding gown, her face hidden behind a gossamer veil.

The watchman called out, offering assistance, but the figure remained motionless. As he approached, a feeling of unnatural cold enveloped him, despite the ever-present warmth of the hammam. When he was just a few steps away, the bride slowly raised her head. The watchman froze as she lifted her veil, revealing not the face of a young woman, but a skull with empty eye sockets that seemed to stare directly into his soul. In the next instant, the apparition vanished, leaving the terrified man alone in the echoing chamber.

This encounter, whether truth or embellishment, cemented Ayşe's place in the folklore of Istanbul. The Çemberlitaş Hammam became known not just for its historical significance and luxurious baths, but as a place where the veil between the world of the living and the dead grew thin.

Yet not all the stories surrounding Ayşe's ghost were frightening. Many spoke of her as a benevolent spirit, a guardian of the hammam and its patrons. Young brides who visited the bathhouse before their weddings would often leave small offerings - a flower, a piece of candy, or a coin - in quiet corners, asking for Ayşe's blessing on their marriages. Some even claimed that those who gained Ayşe's favor would be granted a long and happy union.

Over time, the legend of the ghostly bride became intertwined with the identity of the Çemberlitaş Hammam itself. Tour guides included the tale in their narratives, drawing eager visitors hoping to catch a glimpse of the supernatural. Skeptics dismissed the story as nothing more than a clever marketing ploy, while believers insisted that there are some things in this world that defy rational explanation.

The hammam's management, for their part, neither confirmed nor denied the ghostly rumors. They simply smiled enigmatically when asked and reminded visitors that the bathhouse's history held many secrets, some of which were best left undisturbed.

As the centuries passed, the legend of Ayşe evolved, taking on new details and significance. In the 1800s, during a time of modernization and change in the Ottoman Empire, the story was sometimes used as a cautionary tale about the dangers of abandoning traditional ways too quickly. In the early 20th century, as women's rights became a topic of discussion, some retold Ayşe's story as a tragedy of a life cut short before she could realize her full potential.

. . .

Today, the Çemberlitaş Hammam continues to operate, offering visitors a glimpse into the past and a unique cultural experience. The marble slabs are still heated from below, the domed ceilings still echo with the sound of running water and conversation, much as they did in Ayşe's day. And while the modern world has encroached in many ways - electric lights have replaced oil lamps, and tourists with cameras are a common sight - there remains an air of timelessness within the hammam's walls.

Late at night, when the last guests have gone and the steam begins to dissipate, it's easy to imagine how the hammam might have looked centuries ago. In those quiet moments, even the most hard-ened skeptic might find themselves straining their ears for the sound of phantom footsteps or the rustle of a bridal gown.

Is the ghost of Ayşe real? Perhaps she is nothing more than a story, a way for people to connect with the past and add a touch of mystery to their lives. Or perhaps, in some inexplicable way, the echoes of a tragedy long past do linger in places of significance.

What is certain is that the legend of the ghostly bride of Çemberlitaş Hammam has become an integral part of Istanbul's rich cultural tapestry. It serves as a reminder that behind every ancient building and weathered stone, there are human stories of love, loss, and the enduring power of memory. In a city where the past and present coexist in every street and alleyway, Ayşe's tale continues to captivate, ensuring that a young bride who died centuries ago will never be truly forgotten.

10

THE MIRACLE OF THE EYÜP SULTAN MOSQUE

The Eyüp Sultan Mosque stands as a beacon of faith and hope on the shores of the Golden Horn, its minarets reaching skyward as if to touch the heavens themselves. For centuries, this sacred site has drawn pilgrims and wishers from across Istanbul and beyond, all seeking the blessings associated with one of the city's most revered figures: Eyüp Al-Ansari, a close companion of the Prophet Muhammad.

. . .

The story of the mosque begins in the 7th century, long before Istanbul was the sprawling metropolis it is today. Eyüp Al-Ansari, a man known for his wisdom and devotion, accompanied the Arab armies that laid siege to Constantinople in 674 CE. Though the siege was unsuccessful, Eyüp remained in the area, continuing to spread the message of Islam until his death. He was buried outside the city walls, his grave marked only by a simple stone.

For centuries, the location of Eyüp's tomb was lost to time, known only through legends and whispered stories passed down through generations. It wasn't until the Ottoman conquest of Constantinople in 1453 that the site was rediscovered, thanks to a mystical vision experienced by Akşemseddin, the spiritual advisor to Sultan Mehmet the Conqueror.

According to the tale, Akşemseddin had a dream in which the location of Eyüp's tomb was revealed to him. Led by this divine guidance, he brought the Sultan to a spot just outside the city walls. There, they uncovered the ancient grave, and the Sultan immediately ordered the construction of a mosque and mausoleum complex to honor the memory of this revered figure.

The Eyüp Sultan Mosque quickly became one of the most important religious sites in the Ottoman Empire. Its proximity to the city walls made it the first stop for sultans embarking on military campaigns, where they would pray for victory and symbolically gird themselves with the Sword of Osman in a ceremony marking their ascension to the throne.

But it wasn't just sultans who sought the blessings of Eyüp Sultan. Ordinary people flocked to the mosque, drawn by stories of miracles and answered prayers. Over time, a particular ritual emerged that captured the imagination of the faithful and continues to this day: the tying of threads to the golden grille surrounding Eyüp's tomb.

The origins of this practice are shrouded in mystery. Some say it began with a dream, others with a spontaneous act of devotion that spread by word of mouth. Regardless of how it started, the ritual soon became an integral part of visits to the mosque.

The process is simple yet profound. Pilgrims approach the ornate golden grille that encloses the tomb of Eyüp Al-Ansari. With reverence, they tie a small thread or piece of string to the metalwork, all the while focusing intently on their deepest wish or prayer. It might be for health, for love, for success in business or studies - the nature of the wish is as varied as the people who come to make them.

But the tying of the thread is only the beginning. The true miracle, it's said, occurs when the wish is granted. At that moment, believers claim, the thread will untie itself and fall away from the grille, a physical manifestation of the fulfillment of one's heart's desire.

This belief has led to some remarkable scenes at the mosque. On any given day, one can see people of all ages and backgrounds carefully examining the grille, looking for their thread among the hundreds tied there. Some come daily, hope etched on their faces as they search for a sign that their prayers have been answered. Others return after months or even years, amazed to find their thread gone, taking it as confirmation that their wish has indeed come true.

. . .

The power of this ritual lies not just in the possibility of wishes granted, but in the hope it instills. For many, the act of tying the thread is a way of making their innermost desires tangible, of taking a step towards making their dreams a reality. It's a physical representation of faith, a reminder that even in the face of seemingly insurmountable odds, there is always room for hope.

Over the years, countless stories have emerged of wishes fulfilled through this miraculous thread. There are tales of the sick being cured, of long-lost loved ones reunited, of fortunes reversed and dreams achieved. Whether these outcomes are the result of divine intervention, the power of positive thinking, or simply the natural ebb and flow of life's circumstances is a matter of personal belief. But for those who have experienced it, the miracle of the untying thread is undeniably real.

One such story tells of a young woman named Ayşe, who had been trying unsuccessfully for years to have a child. After exhausting all medical options, she came to the Eyüp Sultan Mosque as a last resort. With tears in her eyes, she tied her thread to the grille, pouring all her hopes and fears into that simple act. Months passed, and Ayşe continued to visit the mosque, her faith unwavering despite the lack of change in her situation. Then, on a sunny spring morning almost a year after she first tied her thread, Ayşe approached the grille and found her string lying on the ground, untied. A week later, she discovered she was pregnant.

Another legend speaks of a poor student named Mehmet, who dreamed of becoming a great scholar but lacked the means to continue his education. He tied his thread to the grille, wishing for a way to pursue his studies. Days later, a wealthy merchant overheard Mehmet reciting poetry in a coffee house and was so impressed by the young man's intelligence and passion that he offered to sponsor his education. When Mehmet returned to the mosque to give thanks, he found his thread had vanished.

These stories and countless others like them have cemented the reputation of the Eyüp Sultan Mosque as a place where miracles happen. But the impact of this belief extends far beyond the individual wishes granted. The mosque has become a symbol of hope for the entire city, a place where the impossible becomes possible, where faith can move mountains - or at least untie threads.

The ritual has also fostered a sense of community among those who participate. Strangers strike up conversations as they search for their threads, sharing their hopes and experiences. People who have had their wishes granted often return to tie new threads for others, paying forward the blessings they've received. In this way, the golden grille has become more than just a focal point for individual prayers; it's a tapestry of shared hopes and dreams, woven together by thousands of tiny threads.

Of course, not everyone views the untying threads as miraculous. Skeptics point out that in a busy mosque with thousands of visitors, it's inevitable that threads will come loose or be accidentally untied. They argue that people are simply seeing what they want to see, attributing natural occurrences to supernatural causes.

But for believers, these rational explanations miss the point. The power of the ritual, they say, lies not in the physical act of the thread untying, but in the faith and hope it represents. The thread is a symbol, a tangible connection between the earthly and the divine. Whether it falls away through miraculous intervention or mundane means is less important than the change it inspires in the hearts and minds of those who participate.

. . .

As Istanbul has grown and changed over the centuries, the Eyüp Sultan Mosque has remained a constant, a touchstone for generations of residents and visitors. The practice of tying wishes to the grille has evolved as well, adapting to the modern world while retaining its essential spirit. Today, alongside traditional threads, one might see ribbons, strips of cloth, or even carefully folded papers tied to the metalwork, each representing a hope, a dream, a silent prayer.

The mosque itself has undergone renovations and expansions over the years, but great care has always been taken to preserve the tomb of Eyüp Al-Ansari and the golden grille that surrounds it. The current grille, an intricate work of art in gleaming gold, was installed in the 19th century, replacing an older silver one. Its ornate design, featuring geometric patterns and calligraphic inscriptions, serves as a fitting backdrop for the thousands of wishes tied to it each year.

Beyond its religious significance, the Eyüp Sultan Mosque and its miracle-working grille have become an integral part of Istanbul's cultural landscape. The ritual of tying threads has been featured in novels, films, and songs, cementing its place in the popular imagination. It's not uncommon to see characters in Turkish TV dramas making a pilgrimage to the mosque in times of crisis, tying their thread with tearful determination.

For visitors to Istanbul, a trip to the Eyüp Sultan Mosque offers a glimpse into the living, breathing faith that has shaped the city for centuries. The sight of the golden grille, festooned with countless threads and ribbons, each representing a heartfelt wish, is a powerful reminder of the human capacity for hope and the enduring nature of faith.

As the sun sets over the Golden Horn, casting a warm glow over the mosque's white marble facade, the faithful continue to come. They tie their threads, whisper their prayers, and leave with hearts lightened by the possibility of miracles. And who knows? Perhaps, in this ancient place where the veil between the earthly and the divine seems just a little bit thinner, wishes really do come true.

11

THE THREE COLUMNS

In the heart of Istanbul's old city, stand three columns that have captured the imagination of locals and visitors for centuries. Each bears its own legend, a story that blends history and myth, fact and fantasy. Together, they form a trinity of mystery that speaks to the enduring magic of this timeless city.

The first of these, the Serpent Column, rises from the center of the ancient Hippodrome, now known as Sultanahmet Square. At first glance, it might not seem impressive - a twisted bronze pillar, worn by time and the elements. But this column has a history that stretches back over two and a half millennia, to a time when the gods of Olympus still held sway over the minds of men.

Originally, the Serpent Column stood in Delphi, Greece, where it was erected to commemorate the Greek city-states' victory over the Persians at the Battle of Plataea in 479 BCE. It once stood nearly six meters tall, crowned with three serpent heads supporting a golden tripod. The names of the 31 Greek cities that fought against the Persians were inscribed on its coils, a testament to their unity and triumph.

But it's not just its age that makes the Serpent Column remarkable. According to legend, it possessed a power far beyond that of a mere monument. The people of Istanbul long believed that the column had the ability to ward off snakes from the city. In a time when venomous reptiles posed a real threat to urban life, this was no small matter.

The story goes that as long as the Serpent Column stood intact, no snake would dare enter the city limits. The bronze serpents atop the column were said to be eternally vigilant, their unseeing eyes scanning the horizon for any slithering intruders. Some even claimed that on quiet nights, one could hear a faint hissing emanating from the column, as if the metal snakes were communicating with their living counterparts, warning them to stay away.

This protective power was taken so seriously that when one of the serpent heads disappeared in the 17th century (some say it was struck by a drunken Polish nobleman, others claim it was removed by a superstitious sultan), there was genuine fear that snakes would once again plague the city. While no sudden infestation occurred, the legend persisted, with many attributing the continued absence of snakes to the column's lingering magic.

Today, the Serpent Column stands as a silent witness to the passage of time, its mystical reputation largely forgotten by all but the most superstitious. Yet for those who know its story, it remains a potent symbol of the city's layered history and the enduring power of belief.

Just a stone's throw from the Serpent Column, within the awe-inspiring depths of Hagia Sophia, we find our next two legendary pillars: the Whirling Columns and the Weeping Column. These marble giants, which have supported the great dome for nearly 1500 years, are steeped in their own mystical lore.

The Whirling Columns, also known as the Wishing Columns, stand in the northwest corner of the massive structure. At first glance, they appear no different from the dozens of other columns that line the interior. But according to legend, these pillars hold a secret power, one that can be unlocked by those who know the right technique.

The ritual is simple but specific. One must approach the column and find a small, damp hole in its surface. Placing their thumb in this hole, they must then attempt to rotate their hand in a full circle. If successful, it's said that the column itself will begin to spin, and the wish made during this rotation will come true.

For centuries, visitors to Hagia Sophia have attempted this feat, their thumbs polishing the marble smooth around the hole. Some claim to have felt the massive pillar tremble beneath their touch, as if it were about to break free from its moorings and twirl like a dervish. Others insist they've seen the column rotate slowly, defying all laws of physics and reason.

Skeptics, of course, argue that any perceived movement is merely the result of dizziness from spinning one's own body around the column. But for those who believe, the Whirling Columns represent a direct line to the divine, a way to send one's deepest desires spinning up to the heavens.

Not far from the Whirling Columns, we find the third member of our mysterious trio: the Weeping Column. Also known as the Wishing Column or the Sweating Column, this pillar is said to possess healing powers that have drawn pilgrims for centuries.

The column's surface is covered with a small bronze plate, worn smooth by countless hands. A hole in this plate reveals the damp marble beneath, which perpetually "weeps" a small amount of moisture. This water, cool to the touch and glistening in the dim light of the great church, is believed by many to be holy, imbued with miraculous healing properties.

The legend of the Weeping Column dates back to the time of Justinian the Great, the Byzantine emperor who built Hagia Sophia. It's said that he once rested his head against this very pillar, seeking relief from a severe headache. To his amazement, the pain disappeared, and the column began to weep, as if sharing in the emperor's earlier distress.

· · ·

Since then, people have flocked to the Weeping Column, hoping to benefit from its purported healing powers. The ritual is simple: one places their finger in the hole, touching the damp marble within, then rubs the affected part of their body with the moistened digit. Ailments from minor aches to serious diseases are said to have been cured by this simple act of faith.

Over the centuries, the legend of the Weeping Column has grown and evolved. Some say the column weeps for the fall of Constantinople to the Ottoman Empire in 1453. Others believe it sheds tears of joy at the unity of faiths represented in Hagia Sophia's long history as both a church and a mosque. There are even those who claim that the column's tears are a warning of future calamities, and that they will flow more freely in times of impending danger.

What's certain is that the Weeping Column, like its whirling neighbors and the snake-warding pillar in the Hippodrome, has become an integral part of Istanbul's mythical landscape. These columns, each with its own unique legend, serve as touchstones for the city's complex history and diverse spiritual traditions.

They remind us that Istanbul is a city where the miraculous and the mundane have always coexisted, where ancient magic lingers in the shadows of modern life. In a place where empires have risen and fallen, where cultures have clashed and melded, perhaps it's not so strange to believe that a column might spin, or weep, or keep an entire city safe from serpents.

For the people of Istanbul, these legends are more than just stories. They're a living connection to the past, a way of touching the intangible threads of history that weave through their daily lives. Each person who presses their thumb to the Whirling Column, or touches the cool moisture of the Weeping Column, or glances up at the Serpent Column while hurrying across Sultanahmet Square, becomes part of this ongoing story.

In a city that has seen so much change, where the modern and the ancient stand side by side, these columns and their legends offer a sense of continuity. They speak to the human need for wonder, for a belief in something beyond the ordinary. Whether one sees them as relics of a more superstitious age or as vessels of genuine mystical power, their impact on the cultural fabric of Istanbul is undeniable.

As the sun sets over the Bosphorus and the call to prayer echoes across the city, these three columns stand as they have for centuries, keepers of secrets both ancient and ongoing. In their weathered surfaces and the stories that cling to them, we can read the complex history of Istanbul itself - a place where every stone has a story, and where the line between legend and reality is as fluid as the waters that surround the city.

For those who know where to look, who have ears to hear the whispers of the past, Istanbul remains a city of marvels. And at its heart, three columns continue to spin, and weep, and ward off serpents, their magic as potent now as it ever was in ages past.

12

———

THE SUNKEN PALACE

Beneath the streets lies a hidden world, a vast underground chamber that has captivated imaginations for centuries. The Basilica Cistern, known in Turkish as Yerebatan Sarnıcı, or "Sunken Cistern," is a marvel of Byzantine engineering. But it's not just its impressive architecture that draws visitors from around the world. It's the legends that swirl around this subterranean wonder, chief among them the tale of the Sunken Palace.

. . .

Built in the 6th century during the reign of Emperor Justinian I, the Basilica Cistern was designed to provide water to the Great Palace and surrounding buildings. Its construction was a feat of ambition and skill, with 336 marble columns supporting a vaulted ceiling over a space that could hold up to 80,000 cubic meters of water.

For centuries, the cistern served its purpose quietly, hidden beneath the city's foundations. But as empires rose and fell, as Constantinople became Istanbul, the true nature of this underground marvel began to fade from memory. It was rediscovered in the modern era almost by accident, when locals reported catching fish through holes in their basement floors.

This rediscovery sparked the imagination of the city's inhabitants. How could such a vast structure have been forgotten? What secrets might it hold? It was in this atmosphere of mystery and wonder that the legend of the Sunken Palace began to take shape.

According to the tale, the Basilica Cistern was not always just a water storage facility. Long ago, it was said, a magnificent palace stood on this spot, home to a Byzantine emperor whose name has been lost to time. This emperor was known for his love of luxury and his fear of assassination. Paranoid about potential threats, he commissioned a palace unlike any other - one that could be submerged underwater at a moment's notice.

The construction of this underwater refuge was a closely guarded secret. The finest architects and engineers were brought in, sworn to secrecy on pain of death. They designed a palace of unparalleled beauty, with halls of marble and gold, intricate mosaics, and windows of crystal that would allow light to filter through the water.

The mechanism for submerging the palace was ingenious. At the pull of a lever, hidden floodgates would open, allowing water from the nearby Bosphorus to rush in, filling the chamber and protecting the emperor from any would-be assassins. The palace was equipped with secret air pockets and passages that would allow the emperor and his chosen few to survive underwater for extended periods.

For years, the emperor lived in his extraordinary home, secure in the knowledge that he could vanish beneath the waves at any sign of danger. But his paranoia only grew with time. He began to suspect everyone around him, even those closest to him. In his madness, he saw assassins in every shadow, heard whispers of conspiracy in every corner.

One fateful night, driven by his delusions, the emperor activated the submersion mechanism. Water poured into the palace, rising rapidly. But in his haste and fear, he had failed to alert his staff or family. As the waters rose, panic ensued. Courtiers and servants scrambled for the exits, but few knew of the secret escape routes. The emperor himself, realizing his mistake too late, was unable to reach safety in time.

By morning, the palace was gone, submerged beneath the streets of the city. Those who survived told tales of the emperor's folly, of the beautiful palace now lost to the depths. Over time, as the truth faded into legend, the story grew and changed. Some said the ghosts of those who drowned still wandered the submerged halls.

Others claimed to hear the faint strains of music drifting up from below, the last echoes of a long-ago court celebration.

As the centuries passed, the legend of the Sunken Palace became intertwined with the real history of the Basilica Cistern. The massive columns, rising from the water like the pillars of a great hall, seemed to lend credence to the tale. Visitors would peer into the dim, watery depths, imagining they could see the outlines of submerged towers or the glint of gold beneath the surface.

The reality, of course, was somewhat different. The Basilica Cistern had always been just that - a cistern, designed for water storage. But the power of the legend was such that it transformed the way people saw and experienced this ancient structure.

When the cistern was opened to the public in the 1987, it was the legend of the Sunken Palace that drew many visitors. Tourism officials, recognizing the appeal of the story, did little to discourage it. Subtle lighting was installed, creating mysterious reflections on the water's surface. Walkways were constructed that allowed visitors to explore the cistern, imagining themselves in the halls of a submerged royal residence.

The presence of unusual features within the cistern only added to its mystique. In the far corner stand two column bases carved with the visage of Medusa, one sideways and one upside-down. These recycled pieces, likely taken from an older Roman structure, became the subject of their own legends. Some linked them to the Sunken Palace story, claiming they were part of a spell to protect the underwater refuge.

· · ·

Another striking feature is the "Wishing Column," a column engraved with tears. According to local lore, touching this column with a damp thumb and rotating your hand can grant your wish. This tradition, while not directly related to the Sunken Palace legend, adds to the cistern's reputation as a place of mystery and magic.

As word of the Basilica Cistern and its legends spread, it began to capture the imagination of artists and storytellers around the world. It has been featured in novels, films, and even video games, each new interpretation adding layers to the myth of the Sunken Palace.

One popular addition to the legend suggests that the palace was not built by a paranoid emperor, but as a refuge for the city's population in times of siege. According to this version, the entire population of Constantinople could supposedly survive for months in the submerged palace, emerging only when the danger had passed.

Another variation claims that the palace was built not by a Byzantine emperor, but by a powerful sorcerer who used magic to create an underwater realm. In this telling, the columns are actually petrified giants, bound by the sorcerer's spells to support the ceiling for eternity.

Despite the fantastic nature of these tales, they speak to a deeper truth about the Basilica Cistern and Istanbul itself. This is a city where the past is always present, where ancient wonders lie hidden beneath modern streets. The legend of the Sunken Palace, with its blend of history and fantasy, captures the essence of Istanbul's enduring mystery.

. . .

Today, as visitors descend the worn stone steps into the cool, dim interior of the Basilica Cistern, they're stepping into more than just an ancient water storage facility. They're entering a space where reality and legend blur, where the weight of history is palpable in the damp air and the soft lapping of water against stone.

The columns, stretching into the gloom, do indeed resemble the pillars of a great hall. The water, reflecting the soft lighting, creates illusions of depth and movement. It's easy, standing on the raised walkways, to imagine that you're exploring the upper levels of a submerged palace, with untold wonders hidden in the depths below.

For many, the appeal of the Basilica Cistern lies in this ambiguity, this space between the real and the imagined. It's a place that invites contemplation, that sparks the imagination. Each visitor becomes, in a sense, a part of the ongoing legend, adding their own interpretations and experiences to the centuries-old story.

The Sunken Palace may be a myth, but the wonder it inspires is very real. In a world where so much is known and catalogued, where mystery often seems in short supply, places like the Basilica Cistern remind us of the power of legend. They invite us to look beyond the surface, to imagine the extraordinary hidden within the ordinary.

As you emerge from the cistern, blinking in the bright Istanbul sunlight, the legend of the Sunken Palace stays with you. It colors your perception of the city, making you wonder what other secrets might lie beneath your feet. In this way, the legend does more than just entertain - it changes how we see and experience the city itself.

The Basilica Cistern and its legend of the Sunken Palace stand as a testament to Istanbul's enduring ability to surprise and enchant. In this city where empires have risen and fallen, where cultures have clashed and melded, the line between history and myth is often blurred. And perhaps that's as it should be. For in the end, it's not just the facts of history that shape a place, but the stories we tell about it, the legends that capture our imaginations and refuse to let go.

13

THE CURSE OF JUSTINIAN

The Hagia Sophia stands as a testament to the grandeur of Byzantine architecture, its massive dome seemingly suspended in mid-air, defying the laws of physics. But within its hallowed halls, a legend persists that speaks to the building's mystical nature and the powerful personality of its creator, Emperor Justinian I.

.   .   .

As the story goes, when Justinian completed the construction of Hagia Sophia in 537 AD, he was overcome with pride. The building was a marvel, unlike anything the world had ever seen. Its vast central dome, intricate mosaics, and forest of marble columns were a testament to the glory of his reign and the might of the Byzantine Empire.

But pride, as they say, often comes before a fall. In his exultation, Justinian is said to have exclaimed, "Solomon, I have surpassed thee!" referencing the biblical king known for building the great temple in Jerusalem. This boast, while perhaps understandable given the magnificence of Hagia Sophia, was seen by many as an act of hubris, a dangerous challenge to divine authority.

Realizing the potential consequences of his words, Justinian sought a way to protect his masterpiece from the jealousy of both gods and men. He decided to implement a curse, one that would guard the secrets of Hagia Sophia's construction and preserve its mystery for generations to come.

The curse was simple yet effective: anyone who managed to count all the columns in Hagia Sophia would be doomed to a terrible fate. Some versions of the legend say the counter would be struck blind, others that they would be driven mad, and still others that they would be cursed with eternal life, forced to wander the earth forever, unable to rest.

At first glance, the task of counting the columns might not seem particularly daunting. After all, how hard could it be to tally up a bunch of marble pillars? But Hagia Sophia is no ordinary building. Its interior is a complex maze of naves, galleries, and hidden corners. Columns of various sizes are everywhere, some prominently displayed, others tucked away in shadowy recesses.

Moreover, the number of columns seems to shift depending on how one defines a column. Are the half-columns embedded in the walls to be counted? What about the smaller columns in the upper galleries? The more one tries to pin down an exact count, the more elusive it becomes.

Over the centuries, many have tried to break Justinian's curse. Scholars, adventurers, and the simply curious have all attempted to tally the columns, each convinced they would be the one to unlock the building's secrets. Some approached the task methodically, marking each column as they went. Others tried to outsmart the curse by counting in teams, reasoning that the curse couldn't affect them all.

One tale speaks of a brilliant mathematician from the 9th century who devised a complex formula to calculate the number of columns without directly counting them. He spent months measuring the building, creating detailed diagrams, and poring over architectural treatises. On the night he was to announce his findings, he mysteriously disappeared. His calculations were found scattered across his study, the final number conspicuously absent.

Another legend tells of a group of Venetian merchants in the 13th century who, seeking to replicate Hagia Sophia's grandeur in their own city, attempted to count the columns. They split into teams, each taking a section of the building. As they compared notes afterwards, they found to their bewilderment that each team had arrived at a different total. Arguments broke out, friendships were shattered, and their grand plans for Venice came to nothing.

Perhaps the most tragic tale is that of a young Ottoman architect in the 16th century. Fascinated by Hagia Sophia's construction, he became obsessed with uncovering its secrets. He spent years studying the building, making countless sketches and measurements. Finally, convinced he had found a way to count the columns without triggering the curse, he entered the building late one night. He was found the next morning, wandering the streets of Istanbul, his mind shattered. For the rest of his days, he could do nothing but mutter strings of numbers, none of which ever added up to the true count of Hagia Sophia's columns.

As the centuries passed and the world grew more scientific, many dismissed Justinian's curse as mere superstition. In the late 19th century, a team of German engineers undertook a comprehensive survey of Hagia Sophia, determined to solve the mystery once and for all. They approached the task with typical Teutonic efficiency, using the latest measuring devices and cataloging techniques.

For weeks, they combed every inch of the building, from the deepest crypt to the highest gallery. Their leader, a man named Friedrich Schmidt, was confident they would succeed where others had failed. But as the survey neared its end, strange things began to happen. Instruments malfunctioned for no apparent reason. Measurements taken one day would inexplicably change the next. Team members reported odd dreams and a growing sense of unease.

On the final day of the survey, as Schmidt was compiling the results, a freak accident occurred. A sudden gust of wind blew through an open window, scattering the papers containing months of meticulous work. In his haste to gather them, Schmidt tripped and fell, striking his head on a marble column. When he regained consciousness days later, he had no memory of the survey or its results.

The German team's failure only added to Hagia Sophia's mystique. If modern science couldn't solve the puzzle, perhaps there really was something supernatural at work. The legend of Justinian's curse grew stronger than ever, attracting a new generation of would-be column counters.

In the early 20th century, as tourism to Istanbul increased, the curse became something of an attraction in itself. Guides would regale visitors with tales of those who had tried and failed to count the columns, each story more outlandish than the last. Some enterprising tour operators even offered "curse-breaking expeditions," promising a thrilling brush with the supernatural (while carefully ensuring their clients never got close to actually completing a count).

Even in the digital age, Justinian's curse continues to captivate. Online forums are filled with debates about the true number of columns and theories about how to break the curse. Some argue that modern technology like 3D scanning could solve the mystery once and for all. Others insist that such methods would only anger the spirits guarding Hagia Sophia's secrets.

A few years ago, a popular video game featured a mission where players had to count Hagia Sophia's columns while avoiding supernatural traps and obstacles. The game's creators, perhaps wary of the curse themselves, programmed the number of columns to change randomly with each playthrough, ensuring the task could never truly be completed.

But beyond the tales of curses and failed attempts, the legend of Hagia Sophia's uncountable columns speaks to something deeper. It's a reminder of the building's enduring mystery, of the awe it has inspired for nearly 1500 years. In a world where so much can be measured, quantified, and explained, Hagia Sophia stands as a monument to the power of the unknowable.

The curse, whether real or imagined, has served its purpose well. It has preserved Hagia Sophia's secrets, ensuring that each generation finds new wonders within its walls. It challenges us to look beyond the merely physical, to see the building not just as a collection of stone and mortar, but as a living testament to human creativity and divine inspiration.

For those who visit Hagia Sophia today, the legend adds an extra layer of intrigue to an already awe-inspiring experience. As you walk among the columns, feeling the weight of history around you, it's hard not to be tempted to start counting. But perhaps it's better to resist that urge. After all, some mysteries are meant to remain unsolved, some wonders uncounted.

And who knows? Perhaps Justinian's spirit still watches over his greatest creation, ready to unleash his curse on any who would dare to unravel its mysteries. In Hagia Sophia, the line between history and legend, between the physical and the supernatural, remains forever blurred. And that, perhaps, is its greatest magic of all.

14

THE TALE OF THE FLYING CARPET

In the annals of Istanbul's folklore, few tales capture the imagination quite like that of the Flying Carpet. This legend, woven into the fabric of the city's history, speaks of a time when magic and reality intertwined, and the impossible became possible through the power of faith and ingenuity.

The story begins during the reign of Sultan Mehmed IV, a ruler known for his piety and his love of hunting. Despite his devotion to the pursuits of the natural world, Mehmed was also a man deeply committed to his religious duties. Every Friday, without fail, he would make the journey from Topkapi Palace to the Eyüp Sultan Mosque for prayers.

The Eyüp Sultan Mosque, located near the end of the Golden Horn, was not just any place of worship. It was built to honor Abu Ayyub al-Ansari, a close companion of the Prophet Muhammad who had fallen during the first Arab siege of Constantinople in the 7th century. The site of his tomb was rediscovered centuries later, and the mosque built around it became one of the holiest places in the Ottoman Empire.

For Sultan Mehmed, the weekly journey to Eyüp was both a spiritual pilgrimage and a logistical challenge. The distance between the palace and the mosque was considerable, and the narrow, winding streets of Istanbul were often congested. Even with his royal entourage clearing the way, the trip could take hours, eating into time the Sultan felt could be better spent in prayer or attending to matters of state.

It was during one particularly frustrating journey, as the Sultan's procession was held up by a traffic jam caused by a overturned cart of melons, that Mehmed expressed his exasperation to his Grand Vizier. "If only," he sighed, "there was a way to fly above these crowded streets, straight to the mosque."

The Grand Vizier, a clever man always eager to please his sovereign, took the Sultan's words to heart. He summoned the finest craftsmen, the most learned scholars, and the most powerful mystics in the empire to the palace. Their task: to create a means for the Sultan to travel swiftly and safely to his Friday prayers.

· · ·

For weeks, the palace buzzed with activity. Inventors presented flying machines inspired by the wings of birds, only to see their creations plummet from the palace walls. Alchemists concocted potions they claimed would make the drinker as light as air, with results that ranged from embarrassing to disastrous. Magicians performed elaborate rituals, calling upon djinn and other supernatural forces, but to no avail.

Just as the Sultan was about to give up hope, a mysterious figure appeared at the palace gates. He was an old man, his beard white as snow, his robes travel-stained and worn. In his arms, he carried a tightly rolled carpet.

The palace guards initially turned the old man away, but he persisted, claiming he had the solution to the Sultan's problem. Intrigued, Mehmed ordered that the stranger be brought before him.

In the opulent throne room, the old man unrolled his carpet. It was a beautiful piece, intricately woven with patterns that seemed to shift and change as one looked at them. Golden threads formed verses from the Quran around its border, glinting in the light that streamed through the stained glass windows.

"Your Majesty," the old man said, his voice surprisingly strong for one of his apparent age, "this carpet has been in my family for generations. It was given to my ancestor by a djinn, grateful for a kindness done. It has the power to fly, carrying its passenger wherever they wish to go."

. . .

The Sultan was skeptical, but also curious. He had heard tales of flying carpets in the stories of One Thousand and One Nights, but had always dismissed them as fanciful inventions. Yet there was something about the old man's earnest demeanor and the strange, shimmering quality of the carpet that gave him pause.

"Prove it," Mehmed commanded.

Without hesitation, the old man stepped onto the carpet, closed his eyes in concentration, and to the astonishment of all present, began to rise into the air. He glided gracefully around the throne room, maneuvering between columns and chandeliers with ease, before gently landing back in front of the awestruck Sultan.

Mehmed was ecstatic. Here, at last, was the solution to his problem. He immediately offered the old man a fortune in gold for the carpet, but to his surprise, the stranger refused.

"This carpet cannot be bought or sold, Your Majesty," the old man explained. "It can only be given freely, as it was given to my ancestor. I offer it to you now, asking only that you use it wisely and remember the power of faith and kindness."

With those words, the old man bowed deeply and left the palace, disappearing into the crowded streets of Istanbul before anyone thought to follow him.

. . .

From that day forward, Sultan Mehmed IV's journeys to Friday prayers became the talk of the city. Those who happened to look up at the right moment would see a carpet soaring above the rooftops, the Sultan seated cross-legged upon it, his royal robes billowing in the wind.

The sight of the flying carpet inspired awe and wonder among the people of Istanbul. Some saw it as a sign of divine favor, proof that their Sultan was blessed by Allah. Others viewed it with suspicion, whispering that such magic must surely be the work of dark forces.

For Mehmed, however, the carpet was simply a tool, albeit an extraordinary one, that allowed him to fulfill his religious duties more efficiently. He used it not only for his trips to the Eyüp Sultan Mosque but also to visit other parts of his vast empire, surprising local officials with his sudden appearances and gaining a reputation for omnipresence that strengthened his rule.

But the magic carpet, for all its wonder, was not without its challenges. On windy days, the Sultan had to hold on tight to avoid being blown off course. Rain would soak through the fabric, making for uncomfortable journeys. And on one memorable occasion, a flock of startled geese nearly caused a mid-air collision.

Despite these occasional mishaps, the flying carpet became an integral part of Sultan Mehmed's reign. It allowed him to connect with his subjects in ways no previous ruler had, dropping in on remote villages and far-flung outposts of the empire. The carpet became a symbol of his authority, as recognizable as his royal seal.

· · ·

As the years passed, however, Mehmed began to rely more and more on the carpet's magic. He used it not just for necessary travel, but for frivolous trips and to escape the pressures of ruling. His advisors worried that he was becoming disconnected from the realities of governing, too enamored with the view from above.

It was during one such escape that tragedy struck. Flying high above the Bosphorus, lost in thought, Mehmed failed to notice a sudden storm brewing. By the time he saw the dark clouds approaching, it was too late. A powerful gust of wind caught the carpet, sending it tumbling through the air. The Sultan, caught off guard, lost his grip and plummeted towards the churning waters below.

In that moment of terror, as the sea rushed up to meet him, Mehmed had an epiphany. He realized that in his fascination with the magical carpet, he had lost sight of the true miracles: the beauty of the world around him, the loyalty of his subjects, the simple joy of feeling solid ground beneath his feet. He closed his eyes, made his peace with Allah, and prepared for the end.

But fate, it seemed, had other plans. Just as Mehmed was about to hit the water, he felt himself jerked upward. Opening his eyes, he saw that the carpet had swooped down and caught him, mere inches from the surface of the Bosphorus. It deposited him gently on the shore, then rolled itself up tightly and never flew again.

Shaken by his near-death experience, Mehmed took it as a sign. He returned to the palace a changed man, recommitting himself to the duties of rulership and the welfare of his people. The magic carpet was carefully preserved, but never again used for flight. Instead, it was laid out in a special room in the palace, where the

Sultan would sit upon it to meditate and reflect on the lessons he had learned.

In time, the story of Sultan Mehmed's flying carpet became legend. As it was told and retold, new details were added, and old ones changed. Some versions claimed that the carpet was woven from the hair of houris, the beautiful maidens of Paradise. Others insisted that it was not a carpet at all, but a prayer mat that flew by the power of the Sultan's faith.

Today, visitors to Topkapi Palace can see a beautiful old carpet displayed in one of its rooms. Tour guides will tell you that this is the famous flying carpet of Sultan Mehmed IV, preserved for centuries as a reminder of a more magical age. Whether it truly once soared above the minarets of Istanbul is a matter of faith and imagination.

But for the people of Istanbul, the legend of the flying carpet is more than just a fanciful tale. It's a reminder of the city's rich history, of the thin line between the mundane and the miraculous. In a place where East meets West, where the ancient and the modern coexist, perhaps it's not so strange to believe that once upon a time, a carpet could fly.

As you walk the streets of Istanbul, gazing up at the soaring domes and minarets, you might just catch yourself wondering: what if? And in that moment of wonder, the magic of the flying carpet lives on, soaring through the realms of possibility on the wings of imagination.

15

THE DISAPPEARED IMAM

In the labyrinth of the old city, there's a story that still sends shivers down the spines of locals and visitors alike. It's the tale of the Vanishing Imam, a mystery that has puzzled the faithful and the skeptical for generations.

The story begins on a Friday in the late 17th century, at a time when the Ottoman Empire was at its zenith. The mosque in question - some say it was the grand Süleymaniye, others insist it was the more modest Rüstem Pasha - was packed for the midday prayers. The faithful had gathered, as they did every week, to hear the wisdom of their beloved imam.

This imam, whose name has been lost to time, was known throughout Istanbul for his eloquence and his deep understanding of the Quran. People would travel from far and wide to hear his sermons, which were said to touch the hearts of even the most hardened sinners. On this particular Friday, the mosque was more crowded than usual, as word had spread that the imam would be addressing a matter of great importance.

As the call to prayer echoed across the city, the congregation settled into respectful silence. The imam, a man in his fifties with a salt-and-pepper beard and kind eyes, made his way to the minbar, the elevated pulpit from which the sermon is delivered. He climbed the steps slowly, his movements deliberate, as if each step carried great significance.

When he reached the top, he turned to face the congregation. Those nearest to the minbar would later swear that there was something different about the imam that day. His eyes seemed to glow with an inner light, and there was a slight smile on his lips, as if he knew a secret that brought him great joy.

The imam began to speak, his voice resonating through the mosque. His words, as always, were captivating. He spoke of the nature of reality, of the thin veil that separates our world from the next. He talked about the importance of faith, not just in the afterlife, but in the unseen wonders that surround us every day.

. . .

As his sermon reached its climax, the imam's voice grew more passionate. He stretched out his arms, as if embracing the entire congregation, and declared, "The miracles of Allah are all around us, if we only have the eyes to see!"

And then, in full view of hundreds of witnesses, the impossible happened. The imam simply vanished.

One moment he was there, his figure silhouetted against the intricate tilework of the mosque wall, and the next - nothing. No puff of smoke, no flash of light, just a sudden, startling absence where a man had stood just a heartbeat before.

For a few seconds, there was absolute silence in the mosque. Then, chaos erupted. People surged forward, climbing over each other to reach the minbar. But when they arrived, they found... nothing. No trace of the imam, no clue as to where he might have gone. It was as if he had simply ceased to exist.

The disappearance of the imam became the talk of Istanbul. Theories abounded. Some claimed it was a divine miracle, that the imam had been so pure of heart that Allah had simply lifted him bodily into Paradise. Others whispered of djinn, the mysterious spirits of Islamic tradition, suggesting that they had spirited the imam away for some inscrutable purpose.

The more skeptically minded insisted there must be a rational explanation. Perhaps there was a hidden trapdoor in the minbar, or maybe the whole thing was an elaborate illusion designed to test the faith of the congregation. But no matter how thoroughly the mosque was searched, no secret passages were found, and those who had been present swore that what they had seen was no mere trick.

As days turned to weeks, and weeks to months, the mystery only deepened. Not a trace of the imam was ever found. His home, when searched, revealed nothing unusual - just the simple belongings of a man devoted to his faith and his studies. There were no signs of preparation for a journey, no farewell letters, nothing to suggest he had planned to leave.

The imam's family was questioned extensively. His wife, a quiet, dignified woman, insisted that her husband had been his usual self on the morning of his disappearance. He had eaten breakfast, studied his texts, and left for the mosque just as he did every Friday. Their children, equally baffled, could offer no explanation for their father's vanishing act.

As time passed, the story of the Vanishing Imam took on a life of its own. It was told and retold, each iteration adding new details, new interpretations. Some versions claimed that just before he disappeared, the imam had spoken a secret name of God, unlocking the mysteries of the universe. Others insisted that he had been a saint in disguise, testing the faith of his followers.

The mosque where the incident occurred became a site of pilgrimage. People would come from far and wide to stand in the spot where the imam had vanished, hoping to feel some trace of the divine power that must have been at work. Some claimed to experience visions or to hear whispers of otherworldly wisdom when they stood on the minbar.

.   .   .

The story even reached the ears of the Sultan, who ordered an official investigation. But despite the efforts of the empire's finest minds, no explanation could be found. The Sultan, both intrigued and unsettled by the mystery, ordered that a commemorative plaque be placed in the mosque, marking the spot where the imam had last been seen.

As the years went by, the tale of the Vanishing Imam became woven into the fabric of Istanbul's folklore. It was a story parents told their children to illustrate the mysteries of faith. Street performers enacted stylized versions of the disappearance, much to the delight of tourists. Scholars and mystics alike pored over religious texts, seeking some precedent or explanation for the event.

But perhaps the most intriguing development came decades after the imam's disappearance. A group of renovators, working on an old house in a distant quarter of the city, made a strange discovery. Hidden in a secret compartment in the wall, they found a manuscript. It was written in an archaic form of Turkish, its pages brittle with age.

The manuscript purported to be the secret diary of the vanished imam. In it, he spoke of visions he had experienced, of conversations with beings from other realms. He wrote of a growing certainty that our world was just one of many, and that it was possible - with the right knowledge and purity of heart - to step from one to another.

The final entry, dated the day before his disappearance, read simply: "Tomorrow, I will show them the truth of what I have learned. May Allah guide my steps into the unknown."

. . .

The discovery of the manuscript sparked a new wave of interest in the old legend. Scholars argued over its authenticity, while mystics claimed it as proof of their esoteric beliefs. Some dismissed it as an elaborate hoax, while others saw it as the key to unlocking the mysteries of the universe.

To this day, the true fate of the Vanishing Imam remains unknown. Did he indeed find a way to transcend our reality, stepping into some higher plane of existence? Was he the victim of some elaborate plot, or perhaps the perpetrator of one? Or was it all simply a story that grew in the telling, a myth born from some more mundane incident, distorted by time and imagination?

In the narrow streets of old Istanbul, in the shadow of ancient minarets, the legend lives on. Tour guides point out the mosque where it supposedly happened, embellishing the tale for wide-eyed visitors. Old men in tea houses debate the various theories, each convinced that they alone know the truth.

And sometimes, in the hushed stillness of a mosque at twilight, when the last echoes of the call to prayer have faded away, visitors report a strange sensation. They say they can almost hear a voice, soft but clear, speaking of wonders beyond imagining. In those moments, the veil between worlds seems thin indeed, and the story of the Vanishing Imam feels less like legend and more like a promise - a tantalizing glimpse of mysteries yet to be unveiled.

For in Istanbul, a city where the past and present coexist in every cobblestone and minaret, where East meets West and the mundane dances with the miraculous, who's to say what's truly possible? The tale of the Vanishing Imam serves as a reminder that in this ancient city, magic is never far away - if you only know where to look.

16

THE SEVEN HILLS

As city straddling two continents, Istanbul has long been a place where myth and reality intertwine. Among its many legends, one stands out for its grand scale and symbolic power: the tale of the Seven Hills. This story speaks not just to the city's physical landscape, but to its historical and spiritual significance as well.

. . .

The legend begins in the 4th century AD, when Emperor Constantine the Great decided to move the capital of the Roman Empire from Rome to the ancient city of Byzantium. As the story goes, Constantine was drawn to Byzantium not just for its strategic location, but because he saw in its topography a mirror of Rome itself.

Like the Eternal City, Byzantium was built on seven distinct hills. To Constantine, this was a sign from the divine, a celestial nod of approval for his ambitious plan to create a "New Rome" in the East. He set about transforming the modest Greek colony into a magnificent imperial capital, which would come to be known as Constantinople.

The seven hills of Constantinople, much like those of Rome, were not just geographical features. They became the backbone of the city's urban development, each hill crowned with magnificent structures that showcased the empire's power and piety.

As centuries passed and empires rose and fell, the significance of the seven hills evolved. When the Ottomans conquered Constantinople in 1453, they inherited this symbolic landscape. The sultans, eager to stamp their own mark on the city, began a campaign of construction that would transform the skyline.

Where Byzantine churches and palaces once stood, grand mosques now rose towards the heavens. Each of the seven hills became home to an imperial mosque, commissioned by a sultan and designed to outshine all that came before. These mosques were more than just places of worship; they were statements of power, piety, and artistic achievement.

. . .

The First Hill, the site of ancient Byzantium, is crowned by the Topkapi Palace and Hagia Sophia. Once the greatest church in Christendom, Hagia Sophia was converted into a mosque by Mehmed the Conqueror. Its massive dome and intricate mosaics bear witness to the successive waves of history that have washed over the city.

On the Second Hill stands the Nuruosmaniye Mosque, its unique baroque style a testament to the Ottoman Empire's increasing engagement with Western aesthetics in the 18th century. The mosque's name, meaning "The Light of Osman," refers both to its founder, Sultan Osman III, and to the divine light that Muslims believe guides the faithful.

The Third Hill is dominated by the Süleymaniye Mosque, often considered the masterpiece of the great Ottoman architect Sinan. Built for Süleyman the Magnificent, this mosque complex was designed to rival Hagia Sophia in grandeur and surpass it in beauty. Its four minarets, a rarity at the time, signified that Süleyman was the fourth sultan to rule Constantinople since its conquest.

Atop the Fourth Hill sits the Fatih Mosque, built on the site of the Church of the Holy Apostles. This mosque, named after Mehmed the Conqueror (Fatih means "the Conqueror" in Turkish), symbolizes the Ottoman transformation of the Byzantine city. The original 15th-century structure was destroyed in an earthquake and rebuilt in the 18th century, its new design a blend of classical Ottoman and baroque elements.

The Fifth Hill is marked by the Yavuz Selim Mosque, named after Sultan Selim I. Known as "Selim the Grim" for his stern demeanor, this sultan greatly expanded the Ottoman Empire, conquering much of the Middle East and North Africa. His mosque, with its wide central dome and spacious courtyard, reflects the growing confidence and resources of the empire in the early 16th century.

On the Sixth Hill stands the Mihrimah Sultan Mosque, unique among the imperial mosques for being named after a woman. Mihrimah was the daughter of Süleyman the Magnificent and one of the most powerful women in Ottoman history. Her mosque, also designed by Sinan, is known for its delicate proportions and abundant windows that fill the interior with light.

Finally, the Seventh Hill is crowned by the Koca Mustafa Pasha Mosque. Originally a 6th-century Byzantine church, it was converted into a mosque in the late 15th century. Its mixed architectural heritage, with Byzantine foundations and Ottoman additions, serves as a fitting symbol for a city that has always been a meeting point of cultures.

The legend of the Seven Hills and their imperial mosques is more than just a quirk of geography or a neat parallel with Rome. It encapsulates the way Istanbul has absorbed and transformed the legacies of the empires that have ruled it. Each hill tells a story of conquest, conversion, and continuity.

But the significance of the seven hills goes beyond mere symbolism. They have shaped the very way the city has grown and how its residents navigate their daily lives. The hills create natural neighborhoods, each with its own character and history. They offer stunning vistas over the Bosphorus and the Golden Horn, views that have inspired poets and painters for centuries.

. . .

The hills have also presented challenges. Building on such steep terrain required ingenuity, leading to the development of unique architectural solutions. The city's famous stepped streets, winding alleys, and hidden courtyards are all products of its hilly topography.

For visitors to Istanbul, the Seven Hills provide a natural itinerary, a way to explore the city's history and culture through its most prominent landmarks. Climbing these hills, one travels not just through space but through time, each summit offering a different perspective on the layers of history that make up this extraordinary city.

But like many legends, the story of Istanbul's Seven Hills is not without controversy. Geographers and historians have long debated which exact hills make up the sacred seven. The city's topography is complex, with many more than seven distinct elevations. Different sources list different hills, and the boundaries between them are often unclear.

Some scholars argue that the whole concept of Seven Hills is a later invention, an attempt to link Istanbul more closely with Rome and to emphasize its imperial status. They point out that early Byzantine sources don't mention seven hills, and that the idea seems to have gained prominence only in the Ottoman period.

Yet regardless of its historical accuracy, the legend of the Seven Hills has become an integral part of how Istanbul sees itself and how it is seen by the world. It's a story that resonates with the city's residents and captures the imagination of its visitors.

· · ·

In recent years, as Istanbul has expanded far beyond its historical core, the significance of the Seven Hills has taken on new dimensions. For some, they represent a link to the past in a rapidly modernizing city. For others, they're a reminder of the religious and imperial legacies that continue to shape Turkey's identity and politics.

Urban planners and preservationists invoke the Seven Hills in their efforts to protect Istanbul's skyline from unchecked development. They argue that allowing skyscrapers to overshadow the imperial mosques would be a desecration of the city's historical character.

Artists and writers continue to find inspiration in the Seven Hills, using them as a metaphor for Istanbul's complexity and contradictions. In paintings, novels, and films, the hills often feature as silent characters, their presence looming over the human dramas played out in their shadow.

For the millions of tourists who visit Istanbul each year, the legend of the Seven Hills provides a framework for understanding the city's vast and sometimes overwhelming history. Guidebooks and tours often structure their narratives around these seven points, using them as a way to make sense of Istanbul's many layers.

As night falls over the city and the call to prayer echoes from minaret to minaret, the Seven Hills take on a magical quality. The imperial mosques, lit up against the darkening sky, seem to float above the urban sprawl. In these moments, it's easy to believe in the legend, to feel the weight of history and the touch of the divine that the story evokes.

· · ·

The tale of Istanbul's Seven Hills is more than just a quaint local legend. It's a story about how cities create their identities, how geography shapes destiny, and how the past continues to influence the present. In a city that has been the capital of two great empires and a crossroads of cultures for millennia, the Seven Hills stand as silent witnesses to the ebb and flow of history, their slopes echoing with the footsteps of countless generations who have called this remarkable place home.

THE GOLDEN HORN'S CHAIN

The Golden Horn, a natural harbor that has sheltered ships for millennia, holds many secrets beneath its waters. But perhaps none is as intriguing as the tale of the great chain that once spanned its mouth, a formidable defense that kept Istanbul safe from naval invaders for centuries.

The story of the Golden Horn chain begins in the 5th century AD, during the reign of Byzantine Emperor Leo I. Constantinople, as

Istanbul was then known, was a city under constant threat. Its strategic position, straddling Europe and Asia, made it a tempting target for any power seeking to control trade routes between East and West.

The city's land walls, massive structures of stone and brick, were nearly impregnable. But the sea approaches remained vulnerable. The Golden Horn, a natural inlet of the Bosphorus Strait, provided an ideal harbor for the city's fleet. However, it also offered a potential entry point for enemy ships.

Leo I, recognizing this weakness, commissioned the construction of a massive chain that could be stretched across the entrance of the Golden Horn in times of danger. This was no ordinary chain. Each link was forged from iron, thick as a man's arm and heavy enough that it took several strong men to lift even a small section.

The chain was anchored on the northern shore of the Golden Horn, in the area now known as Galata. On the opposite shore, in what is today the district of Sarayburnu, a great tower was built to house the machinery that would raise and lower the chain. When fully extended, the chain created a barrier nearly half a mile long.

In times of peace, the chain lay submerged, allowing merchant ships to pass freely in and out of the harbor. But when danger threatened, it could be raised, creating an impassable barrier. Enemy ships, their momentum suddenly checked by the chain, would be left vulnerable to attacks from the city's defenders.

The first real test of the chain came in 626 AD, during a joint siege by the Avars and the Sassanid Persians. As the enemy fleet approached, the defenders raised the chain. The attackers, unprepared for this obstacle, saw their ships bunched up at the harbor entrance, easy targets for Byzantine fire ships and artillery. The siege was repelled, and the chain proved its worth.

Over the centuries that followed, the chain played a crucial role in numerous sieges and battles. It was constantly maintained and upgraded, with successive emperors recognizing its importance to the city's defenses. The chain became not just a physical barrier, but a psychological one as well. The mere knowledge of its existence deterred many potential attackers.

Perhaps the most famous episode in the chain's history came during the final siege of Constantinople by the Ottoman Turks in 1453. Sultan Mehmed II, determined to capture the city, knew that the chain would prevent his ships from entering the Golden Horn. In a move that would go down in history, he ordered his fleet to be transported overland, bypassing the chain entirely.

Under cover of darkness, Ottoman ships were hauled on greased logs across the hills of Galata, then lowered into the Golden Horn behind the chain. The defenders, waking to find enemy vessels in their supposedly secure harbor, were demoralized. This ingenious maneuver played a significant role in the eventual fall of Constantinople.

After the Ottoman conquest, the chain fell into disuse. The new rulers of the city, confident in their naval supremacy, saw no need for such a defensive measure. Gradually, the great chain sank into the waters of the Golden Horn, its location forgotten as the centuries passed.

.   .   .

But the legend of the chain lived on in the stories told by Istanbul's residents. Fishermen claimed their nets sometimes snagged on massive iron links hidden in the silt at the bottom of the harbor. Divers spoke of glimpsing shadowy shapes that could be the remains of the ancient barrier.

In the 19th century, as interest in Byzantine history grew, scholars began to search for evidence of the Golden Horn chain. Old maps were studied, ancient texts scrutinized. Underwater surveys were conducted, seeking any trace of the massive iron links.

These efforts yielded tantalizing clues. Sections of heavy chain were indeed found on the seabed, though it was difficult to date them conclusively. On the shores of the Golden Horn, archaeologists uncovered what appeared to be the foundations of towers that could have anchored the chain.

But the most exciting discovery came in the early 20th century. During construction work near the old city walls, workers uncovered a massive iron link, far larger than any ordinary chain. Experts who examined it declared that it could very well be a piece of the legendary Golden Horn chain.

This find sparked a renewed interest in the chain and its history. Museums in Istanbul now display sections of chain that may have once spanned the Golden Horn. While their authenticity is debated, they serve as tangible reminders of the ingenuity and determination of the city's ancient defenders.

.   .   .

The story of the Golden Horn chain has captured the imagination of writers, filmmakers, and artists. It features in historical novels set in Byzantine Constantinople, often depicted as a symbol of the city's resilience in the face of seemingly overwhelming odds. In Turkish cinema, the chain and Mehmed II's clever circumvention of it have been portrayed in epic scenes, celebrating Ottoman ingenuity.

For modern-day visitors to Istanbul, the tale of the chain adds an extra layer of intrigue to boat tours of the Golden Horn. Guides point out the spots where the chain was supposedly anchored, inviting tourists to imagine the massive barrier that once spanned the water.

The chain has also become a metaphor in Turkish culture, often used to describe seemingly insurmountable obstacles or clever solutions to complex problems. "Bypassing the chain," in colloquial speech, can mean finding an innovative way around a difficult situation.

Historians and archaeologists continue to debate the details of the Golden Horn chain. How was it constructed? How effective was it really in defending the city? Could remnants of it still lie hidden beneath the waters of the Golden Horn?

Some scholars argue that the importance of the chain has been exaggerated over time. They point out that while it may have been an impressive feat of engineering, it was just one part of Constantinople's complex defense system. Others maintain that the psychological impact of the chain was as important as its physical presence, deterring potential attackers and boosting the morale of the city's defenders.

. . .

What's clear is that the chain represents a remarkable example of ancient military technology. At a time when naval warfare was a crucial aspect of Mediterranean power struggles, the ability to completely seal off a major harbor was a significant advantage.

The chain also speaks to the broader history of Istanbul as a city that has always had to balance openness with security. Located at the crossroads of continents and cultures, it has been a center of trade and exchange for millennia. Yet this same strategic position has made it a target, necessitating innovative defenses like the Golden Horn chain.

In recent years, there have been calls to conduct more thorough underwater archaeological surveys of the Golden Horn, using modern technology to search for any remaining traces of the chain. Proponents argue that such a project could not only shed light on this specific historical artifact but also provide valuable information about Byzantine engineering and metallurgy.

For now, the Golden Horn chain remains partly in the realm of legend. Like many aspects of Istanbul's long and complex history, it blends documented fact with folklore, archaeological evidence with centuries of storytelling. But this ambiguity only adds to its allure.

As the sun sets over the Golden Horn, casting a golden glow across its waters, it's easy to imagine the great chain rising from the depths, link by massive link. In that moment, the centuries seem to fall away, and the ancient city, with all its fears and hopes, its innovations and traditions, feels startlingly present.

.   .   .

The tale of the Golden Horn chain is more than just a historical curiosity. It's a reminder of the ingenuity and determination that have always characterized the people of Istanbul. In a city that has reinvented itself countless times over the millennia, the chain stands as a symbol of continuity - a link, if you will, between past and present.

Whether one sees it as a feat of engineering, a military innovation, or simply a great story, the Golden Horn chain remains an integral part of Istanbul's rich tapestry of legends. It continues to intrigue and inspire, inviting us to look beneath the surface - of both the Golden Horn's waters and Istanbul's history - and imagine the wonders that might still lie hidden there.

18

THE YEREBATAN MONKEY

Beneath the streets of Istanbul, in the cavernous depths of the Basilica Cistern, a peculiar tale has been whispered for generations. It's the story of the Yere Batan Monkey, a mischievous creature that once called this underground wonder its home. This legend, blending history with fantasy, adds an unexpected twist to the already mysterious atmosphere of the ancient water reservoir.

. . .

The Basilica Cistern, known in Turkish as Yerebatan Sarnıcı (meaning "Sunken Cistern"), was built in the 6th century during the reign of Byzantine Emperor Justinian I. With its forest of 336 marble columns rising from dark waters, it has long been a source of fascination and speculation. But it's the story of its simian inhabitant that truly captures the imagination.

According to the legend, sometime in the late Ottoman period, a small monkey appeared in the cistern. No one knew where it came from or how it got there. Some said it escaped from a merchant ship docked in the nearby Golden Horn. Others claimed it was the pet of a wealthy pasha, abandoned when its owner fell from grace. Still others whispered that it was no ordinary monkey at all, but a djinn in disguise, bound to the cistern by ancient magic.

Whatever its origins, the monkey quickly became a fixture in the shadowy world of the Yerebatan. It would swing from column to column, its agile form reflected in the still waters below. Visitors to the cistern, descending the worn stone steps into the cool darkness, would be startled by sudden movements in the gloom or the echo of inhuman chatter bouncing off the vaulted ceiling.

At first, the monkey's presence was seen as a nuisance. The caretakers of the cistern tried to capture it, fearing it would damage the ancient structure or frighten away visitors. But the creature proved too clever and elusive. It seemed to know every nook and cranny of the vast underground chamber, disappearing into shadows whenever anyone got too close.

As time passed, however, attitudes towards the cistern's simian resident began to change. People started to see the monkey as a kind of unofficial guardian of the Yerebatan. Stories spread of it leading lost children back to the entrance or warning visitors away from unstable areas with its cries. Some even claimed that the monkey had saved lives, alerting caretakers to cracks in the cistern's structure before they could lead to catastrophic flooding.

The legend grew, as legends do. Soon, it wasn't just a monkey living in the cistern – it was a monkey guarding an ancient treasure. Tales circulated of Byzantine gold hidden in secret chambers, of magical artifacts concealed beneath the murky waters. The monkey, it was said, was the key to finding these riches. If one could catch it, or perhaps just win its trust, it would reveal the location of the hidden treasure.

This new twist to the story attracted all sorts of adventurers and treasure hunters to the Yerebatan. They would descend into the cistern with nets and traps, hoping to capture the elusive creature. But no matter how elaborate their plans, the monkey always seemed to be one step ahead. It would lead its pursuers on wild chases through the forest of columns, only to vanish without a trace, leaving the frustrated treasure hunters soaked and empty-handed.

The monkey's antics became a source of entertainment for regular visitors to the cistern. People would bring treats, hoping to catch a glimpse of the famous Yere Batan Monkey. Children especially were enchanted by the idea of the playful creature swinging through the eerie underground space. Parents would tell their kids to keep an eye out for a flash of fur or the glint of mischievous eyes in the darkness.

Over time, the monkey took on an almost mythical status. It was said to be impossibly old, having lived in the cistern for centuries.

Some claimed it had been there since Byzantine times, perhaps even placed there by Emperor Justinian himself as a living guardian for the underground reservoir. Others insisted it was immortal, sustained by the magical properties of the cistern's waters.

The legend of the Yere Batan Monkey also became entwined with other myths surrounding the Basilica Cistern. The most famous of these is the story of the Medusa heads used as column bases in one corner of the chamber. According to some versions of the tale, the monkey was the only being able to look directly at these Medusa heads without being turned to stone. It was said that the creature would sit on these columns, staring defiantly into the eyes of the Gorgon, as if daring her to try her petrifying gaze.

As Istanbul modernized in the 20th century, the legend of the Yere Batan Monkey adapted to changing times. When electric lighting was installed in the cistern, making its depths less mysterious, some claimed the monkey had learned to sabotage the lights, plunging unwary visitors into darkness with its mischievous tricks. When tourism to the site increased, there were tales of the monkey pickpocketing distracted sightseers, adding cameras and wristwatches to its fabled treasure hoard.

The story even found its way into popular culture. Local artists created whimsical illustrations of the cistern monkey, often depicting it wearing a fez or swinging from ropes of Turkish delight. Children's books featured adventures of young heroes befriending the clever creature and having underground escapades. A few Turkish films used the legend as a plot device, usually in comedies where bumbling thieves would try to capture the monkey to find the cistern's supposed treasure.

. . .

Of course, there's no historical evidence that a monkey ever actually lived in the Basilica Cistern. The dark, damp environment would be poorly suited to a tropical animal, and the logistics of a monkey surviving there for any length of time strain credibility. Most historians and tour guides treat the story as pure folklore, a colorful tale that adds to the cistern's mystique but nothing more.

Yet the legend persists, evolving with each retelling. In recent years, as environmental awareness has grown, some versions of the story have cast the Yere Batan Monkey as a protector of the cistern's delicate ecosystem. These tales speak of the monkey driving away those who would pollute the waters or harm the fish that live there.

Others have linked the monkey to modern concerns about cultural heritage and conservation. In these tellings, the treasure guarded by the monkey isn't gold or jewels, but knowledge – perhaps ancient texts or blueprints hidden away in the cistern's depths, waiting to be rediscovered.

The enduring appeal of the Yere Batan Monkey legend speaks to the human desire for mystery and magic in an increasingly explained world. In a city as old and storied as Istanbul, where history is layered upon history, such tales find fertile ground. The idea that an ancient underground chamber might house a myste-rious, treasure-guarding monkey captures the imagination in a way that simple historical facts often don't.

Moreover, the legend of the cistern monkey serves as a kind of counterpoint to the grandeur and solemnity of many of Istanbul's historical sites. While places like Hagia Sophia and Topkapi Palace speak to the power of emperors and sultans, the tale of a mischievous monkey swinging through subterranean shadows adds a note of whimsy and folk humor to the city's pantheon of stories.

For visitors to the Basilica Cistern, the legend of the Yere Batan Monkey adds an extra dimension to their experience. As they walk the raised platforms above the dark waters, many find themselves instinctively scanning the shadows for any sign of movement. The story encourages people to engage with the space in a more imaginative way, to see the cistern not just as an architectural wonder but as a place of living legend.

Even those who don't believe in the literal truth of the tale often find themselves caught up in its spirit. It's not uncommon to see tourists tossing coins into the water, half-jokingly making wishes for the monkey to reveal its treasure to them. Some leave small offerings – a piece of fruit, a shiny trinket – as a playful tribute to the cistern's fabled guardian.

The legend has also had some unexpected real-world impacts. It's inspired increased interest in the wildlife that does inhabit the cistern, particularly the fish that swim in its waters. Conservation efforts have been undertaken to protect these creatures, seen by some as the true "treasure" guarded by the spirit of the mythical monkey.

As Istanbul continues to grow and change, the legend of the Yere Batan Monkey serves as a link to the city's past. It's a reminder of a time when the lines between history and myth were more blurred, when underground chambers could house magical creatures and hidden treasures. In a world of smartphones and instant information, there's something appealing about the idea of an elusive monkey guardian, still swinging through the shadows, always just out of reach.

Whether seen as a charming folk tale, a marketing gimmick, or a metaphor for the hidden wonders of Istanbul, the legend of the Yere Batan Monkey has become an integral part of the Basilica Cistern's allure. It adds a touch of the fantastic to the already impressive reality of this underground marvel, inviting visitors to see the space through the eyes of wonder and imagination.

As the waters of the cistern continue to reflect the play of light and shadow from above, who's to say what secrets they might still hide? Perhaps, in some forgotten corner, behind a distant column, a pair of mischievous eyes still watches, guarding treasures both material and intangible, waiting for the right moment to reveal the true wonders of the Yerebatan.

19

THE MARBLE KING

In the winding streets of Istanbul, there's a tale that still captures the imagination of locals and visitors alike. It's the legend of the Marble King, a story of hope, magic, and the enduring spirit of a fallen empire.

The tale begins on May 29, 1453, a date etched into the memory of the city. The Ottoman army, led by the young and ambitious Sultan Mehmed II, had been laying siege to Constantinople for weeks. The once-mighty walls of the Byzantine capital, which had repelled invaders for over a thousand years, were finally crumbling under the relentless assault of Ottoman cannons.

Inside the city, Emperor Constantine XI Palaeologus, the last ruler of the Byzantine Empire, prepared for what he knew would be his final stand. Constantine was a man burdened by history. He bore the name of the city's founder and carried the weight of an empire that had dwindled to little more than the city walls themselves.

As dawn broke on that fateful day, Constantine donned his imperial regalia for the last time. He addressed his remaining troops, his words a mixture of defiance and resignation. "As it has pleased God to grant the enemy entry into our city," he said, "let us face our fate with courage."

The emperor then did something unexpected. He removed his purple boots, emblems of imperial authority, and put on the simple shoes of a common soldier. "If the city falls," he declared, "I will fall with it."

What happened next is a matter of historical debate, but in the realm of legend, the story takes a miraculous turn. As the Ottoman forces breached the walls and poured into the city, Constantine fought valiantly alongside his men. He was last seen near the St. Romanus Gate, sword in hand, facing the oncoming enemy.

But as the legend goes, just as an Ottoman blade was about to strike the emperor, a blinding light filled the air. An angel, sent by God himself, descended upon the battlefield. With a touch, the angel transformed Constantine into a statue of marble, preserving him from death and defeat.

The Ottoman soldiers, bewildered by the emperor's sudden disappearance, surged forward into the city. Constantinople fell, and with it, the last vestige of the Roman Empire. But Constantine, now a marble statue, remained hidden, waiting for the day when he would be needed again.

The legend doesn't end there. It's said that the Marble King was secreted away into a cave beneath the city, a magical chamber that opens to the surface only once every seven years. There, Constantine waits in his marble form, ready to be awakened when the time is right.

How will the Marble King be awakened? The legend provides an answer for this too. It's said that when the time comes for Constantinople to return to Christian rule, a golden-haired boy will be sent by the angels. This boy will find the hidden cave and recite a spell he's been taught. The marble will crack, and Constantine will emerge, as alive and vital as he was on that May morning in 1453.

The resurrected emperor will then lead an army to reclaim the city, driving out the occupiers and restoring the Byzantine Empire to its former glory. The Hagia Sophia, converted into a mosque after the Ottoman conquest, will once again ring with Christian hymns, and the double-headed eagle of Byzantium will fly over the Bosphorus.

This tale of the Marble King quickly spread through the conquered city, offering hope to those who mourned the fall of

Constantinople. It became a symbol of resistance, a promise that their defeat was not final. In the dark years that followed the conquest, many clung to the belief that their emperor would return to liberate them.

The legend evolved over time, absorbing elements from other cultures and traditions. Some versions incorporated the widespread medieval belief in the "sleeping hero" - a great leader who doesn't die but sleeps, waiting to return in his people's hour of need. This motif appears in stories across Europe, from King Arthur in Britain to Frederick Barbarossa in Germany.

In some tellings, Constantine isn't alone in his marble slumber. He's accompanied by a retinue of loyal soldiers, all turned to stone, waiting for the day they'll awaken to fight once more. Other versions claim that the golden-haired boy who will awaken the emperor is actually the reincarnation of Constantine's most trusted general.

The story of the Marble King also became intertwined with other Byzantine legends. One such tale speaks of the Immortal Battalion, a group of soldiers who supposedly guard the tomb of Constantine the Great, the city's founder. In some versions, these immortal warriors will join forces with the awakened Marble King to reclaim Constantinople.

As centuries passed and the Ottoman Empire firmly established its rule over the city, the legend of the Marble King took on new meanings. For the Greek population of Istanbul, it remained a source of cultural pride and a link to their Byzantine heritage. For others, it became a metaphor for the city's resilience and its ability to reinvent itself through countless regimes and empires.

. . .

The tale even found its way into Ottoman folklore. Some Turkish versions of the story cast the Marble King not as a hidden threat but as a guardian spirit of the city, one that would awaken only to protect Istanbul from a greater danger than Ottoman rule.

In the 19th and early 20th centuries, as nationalism swept through the Balkans and the Ottoman Empire began to crumble, the legend of the Marble King gained new political significance. Greek nationalists used it as a rallying cry, a symbol of their hopes to reclaim Constantinople and resurrect the Byzantine Empire.

During World War I, as Allied forces threatened to capture Istanbul, some among the city's Greek population believed the prophecy was about to be fulfilled. There were even reports of people claiming to have seen a marble statue come to life near the old city walls.

The legend has continued to capture imaginations well into the modern era. It's been the subject of novels, poems, and films. Artists have depicted the Marble King in various forms, from classical statuary to modern interpretations that blend Byzantine and contemporary aesthetics.

For visitors to Istanbul, the legend adds an extra layer of mystery to the city's already rich history. Tour guides often include the tale in their narratives, pointing out spots where Constantine was last seen or where the hidden cave might be located. Some even claim that on quiet nights, you can hear the faint sound of marble cracking beneath the streets, as the Marble King stirs in his long slumber.

. . .

Historians and archaeologists, of course, take a more skeptical view of the legend. They point out that there's no historical evidence for Constantine's miraculous transformation or hidden tomb. Most believe that the emperor likely died in battle during the final Ottoman assault, his body lost in the chaos of the conquered city.

Yet even the most hardheaded scholars acknowledge the power of the Marble King legend. It speaks to universal themes of hope in the face of defeat, of justice delayed but not denied. It's a story about the endurance of cultural memory and the human need to find meaning in historical trauma.

In a city like Istanbul, where the past is always present, where ancient ruins stand alongside modern skyscrapers, the line between history and legend is often blurred. The story of the Marble King exists in this liminal space, neither fully fact nor pure fiction, but something in between - a myth that continues to resonate because it speaks to something deep in the human psyche.

Today, as Istanbul grapples with its complex heritage and its place in the modern world, the legend of the Marble King remains relevant. It's a reminder of the city's layered history, of the many cultures and empires that have left their mark on its streets and souls. It challenges us to think about how we relate to the past, how we construct our identities in the face of change.

For some, the Marble King represents a dream of resurrecting past glories. For others, he's a symbol of the city's enduring mystery, a reminder that beneath the surface of the everyday, magic and wonder still exist. And for others still, the legend is simply a great story, one that adds color and depth to their experience of Istanbul.

As night falls over the Bosphorus and the call to prayer echoes from ancient minarets, it's easy to imagine that somewhere beneath the city streets, a marble statue stirs. Whether seen as a promise, a warning, or simply a flight of fancy, the legend of the Marble King continues to be a part of Istanbul's living mythology, a story that, like the city itself, bridges worlds and epochs, always changing yet somehow timeless.

20

THE SEALED CHAMBER IN TOPKAPI PALACE

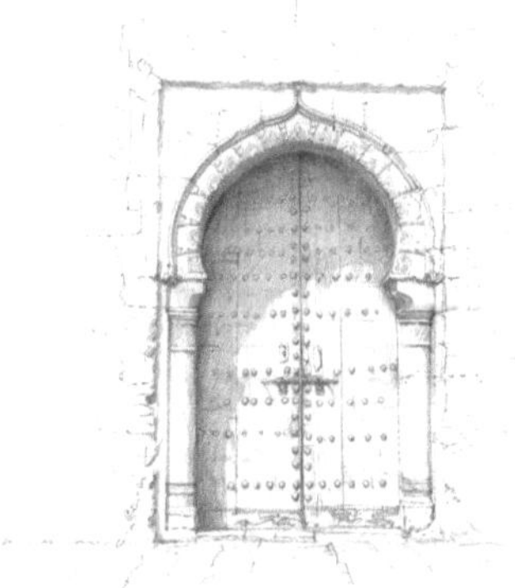

The Topkapi Palace, once the heart of the Ottoman Empire, stands as a testament to centuries of power, intrigue, and mystery. Its sprawling courtyards, ornate chambers, and lush gardens have witnessed the rise and fall of sultans, the whispers of conspiracies, and the unfolding of history. But among the many secrets the palace holds, one has captured the imagination of visitors and locals alike for generations: the legend of the Sealed Chamber.

. . .

Hidden somewhere within the labyrinthine corridors of Topkapi, this mythical room is said to have been sealed by order of Sultan Selim II in the 16th century. The reasons for its closure are as varied as the stories told about its contents. Some say it houses relics of immense religious significance, others claim it contains dangerous ancient knowledge, while still others believe it holds the key to unimaginable wealth.

The tale of the Sealed Chamber begins during the reign of Selim II, known as "Selim the Drunk" due to his fondness for wine, a habit frowned upon in Islamic culture. Despite his reputation for indulgence, Selim was also known for his curiosity and his interest in the esoteric knowledge that had accumulated in the imperial treasury over centuries of conquest and trade.

According to the legend, Selim became fascinated with a collection of scrolls and artifacts that had been gathered by his predecessors. These items, it was said, came from the far corners of the empire and beyond - ancient Greek texts, Egyptian papyri, Persian manuscripts, and even items rumored to have belonged to King Solomon himself.

As Selim delved deeper into these mysteries, he began to experience strange visions and disturbing dreams. Some versions of the story claim that he stumbled upon a prophecy foretelling the fall of the Ottoman Empire, while others suggest he uncovered knowledge so powerful it threatened the very fabric of reality.

Whatever the reason, Selim apparently decided that this knowledge was too dangerous to be left accessible. In a move that baffled his court, he ordered a chamber deep within the palace to be prepared. Into this room went the mysterious scrolls, artifacts, and relics that had so troubled him.

The final step in securing this dangerous knowledge was the most dramatic. Selim commanded that the chamber be sealed not just with locks and bars, but with powerful curses and magical wards. The most skilled Islamic mystics and scholars were summoned to the palace to perform elaborate rituals, ensuring that anyone who attempted to breach the chamber without proper authority would face dire consequences.

With the sealing complete, Selim swore his inner circle to secrecy. The location of the chamber was to be known only to the reigning sultan, passed down from father to son along with the other secrets of rule. Official records of the chamber's existence were destroyed or hidden, leaving only whispered rumors and speculation.

As the centuries passed, the legend of the Sealed Chamber grew. Each generation added its own embellishments to the tale. Some claimed to have seen ghostly lights emanating from hidden cracks in the palace walls, while others spoke of eerie sounds echoing through the corridors on moonless nights.

The contents of the chamber became the subject of endless speculation. Some believed it held the Ark of the Covenant, spirited away from Jerusalem by the Ottomans. Others were convinced it contained alchemical secrets that could turn lead into gold or grant eternal life. There were even those who claimed the chamber housed a portal to other worlds or dimensions, sealed shut to protect our reality from otherworldly invasion.

. . .

The mystery deepened in the 18th century when a series of unexplained events rocked the palace. Servants reported seeing shadowy figures in areas of the palace that had been abandoned for years. Several guards stationed near the rumored location of the Sealed Chamber disappeared without a trace. And during a particularly violent thunderstorm, a portion of an old wall collapsed, revealing a previously unknown passageway that was quickly blocked up on orders from the Sultan.

These incidents led to a renewed interest in the legend of the Sealed Chamber. Some of the more adventurous members of the court began to search for its location, despite the warnings of their elders. A few claimed to have found ancient maps or coded messages that pointed the way, but all such expeditions ended in failure - or worse.

One particularly persistent tale speaks of a young prince who, convinced he had discovered the chamber's location, assembled a group of loyal friends to help him break in. They waited for a moonless night and snuck into the depths of the palace, armed with tools to break through any physical barrier they might encounter.

According to the story, the group successfully located a hidden door that matched the descriptions in the old legends. But as they worked to open it, they were beset by a series of increasingly terrifying supernatural events. Ghostly whispers echoed in the darkness, invisible hands plucked at their clothes, and several members of the group were struck by sudden, inexplicable illnesses.

· · ·

The prince, undeterred, pressed on. But just as he was about to breach the final seal, a blinding light filled the corridor. When it faded, the prince and his companions found themselves back in the main courtyard of the palace, with no memory of how they had gotten there. The prince never spoke of the Sealed Chamber again, and went on to become one of the most pious and conservative sultans in Ottoman history.

As the power of the Ottoman Empire waned in the 19th and early 20th centuries, the legend of the Sealed Chamber took on new significance. Some saw it as a symbol of lost glory, a reminder of a time when the sultans held sway over vast territories and guarded knowledge beyond the understanding of ordinary mortals. Others viewed it as a metaphor for the empire itself - a repository of ancient wisdom and power, sealed away and inaccessible in a changing world.

When the Ottoman Empire finally fell and the last sultan was exiled, many wondered about the fate of the Sealed Chamber. Had its location been lost forever with the end of the imperial line? Or did the secret pass to the new Turkish government?

In the years since Topkapi Palace was converted into a museum, the legend has continued to evolve. Tour guides regale visitors with tales of the chamber, each adding their own spin to the story. Amateur historians and mystery enthusiasts pore over old documents and maps, searching for clues. And every so often, a news story will surface about strange occurrences in the palace, reigniting interest in the centuries-old enigma.

Modern technology has added new wrinkles to the mystery. Ground-penetrating radar surveys of the palace grounds have revealed several anomalies that could be hidden rooms or passageways. These discoveries have led to calls for more thorough investigations, but so far, authorities have been reluctant to allow any destructive exploration of the historic site.

The internet age has also given rise to new theories and claims about the Sealed Chamber. Conspiracy websites are filled with elaborate ideas about its contents, ranging from alien artifacts to time travel devices. Some even claim that the chamber has been secretly opened by shadowy government agencies or powerful secret societies, its contents now hidden in underground vaults or secret laboratories.

Despite the lack of concrete evidence, the legend of the Sealed Chamber continues to captivate. It speaks to our fascination with hidden knowledge, our love of a good mystery, and our enduring belief that there are still secrets waiting to be uncovered in our world.

For the millions of visitors who pass through Topkapi Palace each year, the legend adds an extra layer of excitement to their experience. As they wander through the opulent rooms and peaceful courtyards, many find themselves scanning the walls for hidden doors or listening for ghostly whispers. Even the most skeptical can't help but feel a thrill at the possibility that somewhere, behind these ancient walls, lies a chamber untouched by time, holding wonders beyond imagination.

The Sealed Chamber has also become a popular motif in Turkish literature and film. Novels featuring intrepid archaeologists or modern-day treasure hunters searching for the chamber have become bestsellers. Movies and TV shows have used the legend as a backdrop for everything from historical dramas to supernatural thrillers.

In a way, the enduring appeal of the Sealed Chamber legend reflects Istanbul's own complex relationship with its past. Like the city itself, the tale is a blend of East and West, of historical fact and colorful fiction. It embodies the sense of mystery and potential that still clings to Istanbul, a city where the ancient and the modern coexist in a unique and sometimes uneasy balance.

As night falls over Topkapi Palace and the lights of the city twinkle across the Bosphorus, it's easy to imagine that somewhere in the shadows, behind a wall that has stood for centuries, lies a door unopened since the days of the sultans. What secrets might it hold? What wonders or terrors might be waiting to be unleashed? As long as these questions remain unanswered, the legend of the Sealed Chamber will continue to fire imaginations and draw people to Istanbul, a city where the past is never truly past, and where the next great discovery might be hiding just around the corner.

21

THE BLUE MOSQUE'S COLUMNS

The Blue Mosque, or Sultan Ahmed Mosque as it's officially known, stands as one of Istanbul's most iconic landmarks. Its cascading domes and six minarets pierce the sky, while the intricate blue tiles that give the mosque its popular name dazzle visitors from around the world. But beneath its stunning exterior lies a story of ambition, rivalry, and perhaps a touch of ancient magic.

. . .

Construction of the Blue Mosque began in 1609 under the orders of Sultan Ahmed I. The young sultan, barely 19 years old when he ascended to the throne, was eager to leave his mark on the city. He chose a site directly facing the Hagia Sophia, the greatest church of the Byzantine Empire, in a clear challenge to the older structure's dominance of the Istanbul skyline.

To design and build his grand project, Ahmed turned to Sedefkar Mehmed Agha, a student of the legendary Ottoman architect Mimar Sinan. Mehmed Agha was tasked with creating a mosque that would not only rival the Hagia Sophia in size and beauty but surpass it. It was a daunting challenge, one that would require all of the architect's skill and ingenuity.

As work on the mosque progressed, rumors began to circulate about the extraordinary lengths Mehmed Agha was going to in order to ensure the mosque's perfection. One tale that gained particular traction was that of the ancient columns.

According to the legend, Mehmed Agha wasn't content to use only new materials for the Blue Mosque. He believed that incorporating elements from older, revered structures would imbue the new mosque with a sense of history and spiritual power. To this end, he supposedly sent agents across the Ottoman Empire and beyond, searching for suitable columns from ancient ruins.

The most famous of these columns was said to come from the temple complex at Baalbek in Lebanon. Baalbek, known in Roman times as Heliopolis, was home to some of the largest and most impressive temples in the ancient world. Its massive stone blocks and towering columns had inspired awe for millennia.

·   ·   ·

The story goes that Mehmed Agha's agents identified a particularly magnificent column in Baalbek, one that was said to have stood since the time of King Solomon. Transporting such a massive piece of stone from Lebanon to Istanbul was a monumental task, but one that the determined architect was willing to undertake.

The journey of the Baalbek column, if it indeed took place, would have been an epic undertaking. From the ruins of Baalbek, it would have been carefully lowered and loaded onto a sturdy cart. A team of oxen would have pulled it across the rugged terrain of Lebanon and Syria, a journey of hundreds of miles.

Upon reaching the Mediterranean coast, the column would have been loaded onto a specially reinforced ship. The sea voyage to Istanbul was fraught with danger, from storms to pirates. Some versions of the tale claim that the ship carrying the column was nearly lost in a tempest, saved only by the prayers of the crew who believed in the column's sacred nature.

Finally arriving in Istanbul, the column would have been unloaded and transported up the hill to the construction site of the Blue Mosque. This final leg of the journey, while short in distance, was perhaps the most challenging due to the steep incline and narrow streets of the old city.

But the Baalbek column wasn't the only one with a storied past, according to the legend. Other columns were said to come from various sites across the former Byzantine Empire. Some were supposedly taken from the ruins of Ephesus, the great city of ancient Ionia. Others were said to have come from as far afield as Egypt and even the ruins of Palmyra in the Syrian desert.

. . .

Each of these columns, the story goes, brought with it not just physical support for the mosque's grand domes, but also a piece of the history and spiritual essence of its place of origin. In incorporating these ancient pieces into his new mosque, Mehmed Agha was supposedly creating a structure that was a synthesis of the entire Islamic world.

The legend of the columns added an extra layer of mystique to the already impressive mosque. Visitors would try to identify which columns might be the ancient ones, speculating on their origins and the secrets they might hold. Some even claimed that on quiet nights, when the mosque was empty, you could hear the columns whispering to each other in long-dead languages.

Of course, not everyone believed the tales of the ancient columns. Skeptics pointed out the logistical challenges of transporting such massive stones over such great distances. They argued that it would have been far simpler and more cost-effective to use locally quarried stone for all of the mosque's columns.

Moreover, careful examination of the Blue Mosque's columns reveals a remarkable uniformity in their design and material, suggesting that they were likely all created specifically for this building rather than being a collection of repurposed ancient pillars.

Yet the legend persisted, growing and evolving over time. Some versions of the story claimed that it wasn't just columns that were incorporated into the mosque, but other artifacts as well. There were tales of ancient inscriptions hidden within the walls, of sacred relics embedded in the foundations to provide spiritual protection.

One particularly fanciful version of the legend stated that Mehmed Agha had managed to acquire a piece of the black stone from the Kaaba in Mecca, which he had ground into powder and mixed into the mortar used to set the mosque's foundation stones. While this claim is almost certainly false, it speaks to the way the legend grew to encompass ever more fantastic elements.

The tale of the Blue Mosque's columns also became intertwined with other legends and superstitions. Some believed that touching the Baalbek column could cure illness or bring good fortune. Others claimed that if you listened closely to that column at dawn, you could hear the faint echo of King Solomon's wisdom.

As the centuries passed, the legend of the columns became an integral part of the Blue Mosque's lore. Tour guides would regale visitors with the tale, each adding their own embellishments. The story found its way into travel books and historical novels, further cementing its place in popular imagination.

In the modern era, the legend has taken on new life in unexpected ways. Some New Age spiritual groups have latched onto the idea of the ancient columns, claiming that they form a sort of energy nexus that makes the Blue Mosque a place of special power. These groups sometimes organize meditation sessions or "energy alignment" rituals in the mosque's courtyard, much to the bemusement of other visitors and the mosque's caretakers.

. . .

The tale has also inspired artists and writers. Contemporary Turkish novelists have woven the legend into stories of historical intrigue and supernatural mystery. Visual artists have created works imagining the journey of the columns, from their origins in ancient temples to their final resting place in the Blue Mosque.

For historians and archaeologists, the legend of the columns presents an interesting case study in how myths develop and persist. While there's little evidence to support the idea that the Blue Mosque contains columns from Baalbek or other ancient sites, the story reveals much about how people perceive and relate to historical monuments.

The desire to connect the Blue Mosque to older, revered sites speaks to a human tendency to seek continuity with the past. By imagining that pieces of ancient temples were incorporated into the mosque, people create a tangible link between different eras and cultures. It's a way of seeing history not as a series of disconnected events, but as a continuous flow in which the present is always in dialogue with the past.

Moreover, the legend reflects the Blue Mosque's status as a structure of not just religious but also political and cultural significance. By claiming that it contains elements from across the Islamic world and beyond, the story positions the mosque as a symbol of Ottoman power and influence at its height.

Today, as visitors wander through the grand interior of the Blue Mosque, many still find themselves searching for signs of the legendary ancient columns. While they're unlikely to find any genuine artifacts from Baalbek or Ephesus, what they do discover is perhaps more valuable: a sense of connection to a long and rich history, a feeling of wonder at human creativity and ambition, and a reminder that great monuments are built not just of stone and mortar, but of stories and dreams as well.

As the call to prayer echoes from the Blue Mosque's minarets and the setting sun turns its domes to gold, the legend of the columns serves as a bridge between past and present. It reminds us that in Istanbul, a city where history is always palpable, the line between fact and fiction, between the mundane and the miraculous, is often delightfully blurred. And in that blurring, in that space where imagination meets reality, lies the true magic of this extraordinary city and its magnificent Blue Mosque.

22

THE FISH RESTAURANT'S GHOST

In the Kumkapı district of Istanbul, stands a restaurant that's as famous for its spectral resident as it is for its seafood. The Kumkapı Fish Restaurant, a local institution for decades, is said to be haunted by the ghost of its former owner, a man whose dedication to his establishment apparently transcended the boundaries of life and death.

. . .

The story begins in the 1950s, when Ahmet Efendi, a skilled fisherman turned restaurateur, opened his modest eatery in the heart of Kumkapı. Ahmet was known for his discerning eye when it came to selecting the freshest catch and his talent for preparing traditional Turkish meze. His restaurant quickly became a favorite among locals and tourists alike.

Ahmet's passion for his work was legendary. He would rise before dawn to inspect the day's catch at the fish market, personally selecting each fish that would be served in his restaurant. He was a constant presence in the kitchen, overseeing every dish that left for the dining room. Even after the last customer had gone home, Ahmet could often be found in the restaurant, planning menus or experimenting with new recipes.

As the years passed, Ahmet's restaurant flourished, expanding from a small, family-run operation to a renowned establishment that could seat over a hundred diners. Despite its growth, Ahmet remained hands-on, refusing to compromise on quality or tradition. He trained his staff meticulously, instilling in them his own exacting standards and love for Turkish cuisine.

Ahmet's dedication to his restaurant was so intense that he often joked he would continue running the place even after he died. "They'll have to carry me out feet first," he would say with a laugh, "and even then, I'll be back the next morning to make sure the fish is fresh!"

In the summer of 1985, at the age of 72, Ahmet passed away peacefully in his sleep. His family and staff mourned deeply, wondering how the restaurant would continue without its heart and soul. Ahmet's son, Mehmet, took over the management, vowing to maintain his father's high standards.

It was about a week after Ahmet's funeral that the first strange occurrences were reported. A young waiter, closing up late one night, swore he heard the sound of pots clanging in the empty kitchen. When he went to investigate, he found the kitchen dark and silent, but the lingering scent of Ahmet's favorite fish soup hung in the air.

A few days later, a long-time customer insisted that he had seen Ahmet inspecting the fish display, his brow furrowed in concentration as it always had been in life. When the customer called out a greeting, the figure vanished.

These incidents might have been dismissed as the product of grief and imagination, but they continued to occur with increasing frequency. Staff members reported feeling a presence in the restaurant late at night, as if someone was watching over their shoulders as they worked. The cash register would occasionally open on its own, but never was a single lira missing.

Perhaps the most compelling evidence of Ahmet's continued presence came during a busy Saturday night service. The head chef, a man who had worked alongside Ahmet for decades, was preparing a complex seafood dish when he realized he had forgotten a crucial step in the recipe. As he stood there, momentarily paralyzed by indecision, he felt a gentle tap on his shoulder and heard Ahmet's voice clearly in his ear, reminding him of the missing ingredient. The chef turned, but saw no one. The dish was completed perfectly, just as Ahmet would have made it.

· · ·

As word of these occurrences spread, the Kumkapı Fish Restaurant gained a new kind of fame. Some customers were skeptical, even amused by the tales of the ghostly proprietor. Others were genuinely spooked, requesting tables far from the kitchen where most of the sightings occurred. But many found the idea comforting, believing that Ahmet's spirit was simply continuing the work he had loved in life.

The restaurant's staff, initially unsettled by the paranormal activity, came to accept and even welcome Ahmet's presence. They spoke of feeling protected and guided, especially during busy services or when facing difficult customers. Some claimed that on particularly challenging nights, they would murmur a quiet plea for help, and suddenly the evening would run more smoothly, as if an unseen hand was orchestrating events.

Mehmet, Ahmet's son, was at first reluctant to acknowledge the stories of his father's ghost. He feared it might detract from the restaurant's reputation for excellent food and service. But as the years passed and the incidents continued, he came to embrace the legend. "My father always said this restaurant was his life," Mehmet would tell curious patrons. "Perhaps he meant that more literally than we realized."

The tale of Ahmet's ghost became part of the restaurant's charm, a story shared over plates of grilled sea bass and glasses of raki. It was a testament to the power of passion and the enduring nature of a life well-lived. Customers would raise a toast to Ahmet's memory, half-jokingly asking for his blessing on their meals.

As with many ghost stories, the legend of the Kumkapı Fish Restaurant's spectral owner grew and evolved over time. Some claimed that Ahmet's ghost could be seen walking along the Kumkapı seafront in the early morning mist, inspecting the day's catch before the fishermen had even brought their boats to shore. Others insisted that on quiet nights, the sound of Ahmet's favorite Turkish classical music could be heard drifting from the empty restaurant.

One particularly popular addition to the legend emerged in the late 1990s. A young couple, celebrating their engagement at the restaurant, reportedly saw an elderly man in a white chef's jacket approach their table. He congratulated them warmly and offered them a special dessert "on the house." The dessert, a unique twist on traditional baklava, was delicious. When the couple tried to thank the chef, they were told that no such person worked at the restaurant, and no special dessert had been prepared that night.

The story of Ahmet's ghost even attracted the attention of paranormal investigators. A team from a popular Turkish television show spent a night in the restaurant, armed with cameras and various ghost-detecting equipment. While they didn't capture any definitive evidence of a haunting, several team members reported feeling a strong sense of being watched, and one camera mysteriously malfunctioned in the kitchen, just as they were attempting to communicate with Ahmet's spirit.

Over the years, the Kumkapı Fish Restaurant has changed with the times. The menu has been updated, the decor refreshed, and new generations of staff have come and gone. But through it all, the presence of Ahmet Efendi has remained a constant. His portrait still hangs in a place of honor near the entrance, and many customers make a point of acknowledging it as they enter, some even placing a small offering of flowers or a glass of raki beneath it.

. . .

The legend has had a profound impact on the restaurant's culture. New employees are told Ahmet's story as part of their training, and many report feeling a sense of responsibility to uphold his high standards. There's an unspoken understanding that Ahmet is always watching, ensuring that every dish is prepared with care and every customer is treated with respect.

In recent years, as Istanbul has become an increasingly popular tourist destination, the tale of the Kumkapı Fish Restaurant's ghost has found its way into guidebooks and travel blogs. Visitors from around the world now seek out the restaurant, drawn by the promise of excellent seafood and the possibility of a supernatural encounter.

This newfound fame has brought both benefits and challenges. While business has boomed, there's a constant tension between maintaining the restaurant's authentic character and catering to the expectations of ghost-hunting tourists. Mehmet and his staff work hard to strike a balance, welcoming curious visitors while ensuring that the focus remains on the quality of the food and the preservation of Turkish culinary traditions.

For the people of Kumkapı, the legend of Ahmet's ghost has become a point of local pride. In a rapidly changing city, where old neighborhoods are often lost to development and gentrification, the story provides a link to the past. It's a reminder of the area's long history as a fishing village and a celebration of the hard work and dedication that built its reputation as a culinary destination.

. . .

On quiet winter evenings, when the sea mist rolls in from the Marmara and the streets of Kumkapı are nearly empty, it's easy to imagine Ahmet's ghost making his rounds. Perhaps he pauses at the fish market, nodding approvingly at the day's catch. Maybe he stops to adjust a crooked painting or straighten a tablecloth in his beloved restaurant. And just maybe, if you're lucky enough to be enjoying a late dinner at the Kumkapı Fish Restaurant, you might feel a gentle pat on your shoulder and hear a whispered "Afiyet olsun" - "Enjoy your meal" - from a proprietor whose love for his establishment knew no earthly bounds.

As the legend of the Kumkapı Fish Restaurant's ghost continues to evolve, it serves as a poignant reminder that some passions are strong enough to transcend even death. In a city as ancient and storied as Istanbul, where the line between past and present often blurs, the tale of Ahmet Efendi and his eternal vigil over his beloved restaurant feels not just possible, but somehow right. It's a ghost story, yes, but also a love story - a testament to one man's devotion to his craft, his customers, and the timeless art of bringing people together over a perfect meal.

23

THE UNDERGROUND TUNNELS

Beneath the busy streets of Istanbul, beneath the ancient mosques and bustling bazaars, lies a hidden world that has captivated imaginations for centuries. It's a world of darkness and mystery, of winding passages and forgotten chambers - the legendary underground tunnels of Istanbul.

The story of these tunnels begins in the distant past, long before the city was called Istanbul, when it was still known as Constantinople, the jewel of the Byzantine Empire. As the tale goes, Emperor Constantine the Great, the city's founder, ordered the construction of a vast network of underground passages. These tunnels were meant to serve multiple purposes: as a means of quick and secret transport throughout the city, as emergency escape routes in case of siege, and as hidden storage for treasures and supplies.

Over the centuries, as the city grew and changed hands, the tunnel network supposedly expanded. Each new ruler, from Byzantine emperors to Ottoman sultans, added their own secret passages and chambers. The Hagia Sophia, Topkapi Palace, the Grand Bazaar - all of these iconic landmarks were said to be connected by this subterranean maze.

One of the most persistent legends speaks of a tunnel running beneath the Bosphorus Strait, connecting Europe and Asia. This underwater passage, if it exists, would be an engineering marvel even by today's standards. Yet stories persist of Byzantine emperors using it to make secret diplomatic visits to their Asian territories, and of Ottoman sultans employing it to surprise their enemies with unexpected troop movements.

Another popular tale centers on the Yerebatan Sarnıcı, or Basilica Cistern, a vast underground water reservoir built in the 6th century. According to legend, the cistern was more than just a water storage facility. Secret passages supposedly branched off from its columned halls, leading to hidden chambers where Byzantine emperors could meet in absolute secrecy or escape in times of danger.

. . .

The Ottoman conquest of Constantinople in 1453 added new chapters to the tunnel legends. It's said that the last Byzantine emperor, Constantine XI Palaeologus, used the tunnels in a desperate attempt to rally his troops during the final siege. Some versions of the story claim he disappeared into the underground network, never to be seen again, giving rise to legends that he would one day return to reclaim his city.

Sultan Mehmed the Conqueror, upon taking the city, was allegedly fascinated by the tunnel network. He supposedly expanded it further, creating secret routes between his new palace at Topkapi and key points throughout the city. These passages would have allowed the sultan and his trusted advisors to move about undetected, gathering intelligence or making surprise appearances to keep his subjects and potential rivals on their toes.

As the centuries passed, the legends of the tunnels grew and evolved. During the turbulent years of the late Ottoman Empire, they became the subject of political intrigue. Revolutionaries were said to use the tunnels to hold clandestine meetings and plot against the sultan. Foreign spies supposedly employed them to steal state secrets. Even the mysterious Janissaries, the elite infantry units of the Ottoman army, were rumored to have secret underground training facilities.

The 20th century brought new dimensions to the tunnel stories. During World War I, when Istanbul was under threat of Allied invasion, tales circulated of the Ottoman military using the ancient passages to move troops and supplies undetected. Later, during the Cold War, both Soviet and Western intelligence agencies were said to be obsessed with finding and mapping the tunnel network, seeing it as a potential game-changer in their shadowy conflicts.

. . .

But it's not just political and military figures who feature in the tunnel legends. Over the years, countless stories have emerged of ordinary people encountering the underground network. There are tales of shopkeepers in the Grand Bazaar discovering hidden doors behind their stalls, leading to torch-lit corridors stretching off into darkness. Homeowners renovating old houses in historic neighborhoods report finding bricked-up entrances to mysterious passages.

One particularly popular story tells of a group of children playing in the ruins of an old Ottoman mansion in the 1960s. According to the tale, they found a rusty trapdoor hidden beneath years of debris. Curious, they pried it open and descended into a narrow tunnel. They wandered for what seemed like hours through a maze of passages, eventually emerging, to their astonishment, in the courtyard of Topkapi Palace, miles from where they had entered.

The tunnels have also become entwined with Istanbul's rich supernatural lore. Some believe the passages are haunted by the ghosts of Byzantine emperors or Ottoman sultans, doomed to wander eternally through their underground domains. Others claim that djinn, the mystical beings of Islamic tradition, have made homes in the forgotten chambers beneath the city.

There are even those who link the tunnel legends to more esoteric beliefs. Some occultists claim that the network was designed according to sacred geometries, creating a giant underground mandala that channels mystical energies. Others see connections to ley lines or other theories of earth energies, positioning Istanbul as a major nexus point in a global grid of power.

. . .

Of course, skeptics point out that many of these stories are likely just that - stories. They argue that while Istanbul certainly has its share of underground structures - ancient cisterns, old cellars, abandoned subway tunnels - the idea of a vast, city-wide network of secret passages is probably more fiction than fact.

Historians and archaeologists tend to take a more measured view. They acknowledge that underground passages certainly exist in various parts of the city, some dating back to Byzantine times. The Basilica Cistern and other ancient water management systems are well-documented. There's evidence of tunnels being used for military purposes during various sieges of the city. But they caution against assuming that these disparate underground spaces form a cohesive, intentionally designed network.

Yet the legends persist, capturing the imagination of locals and visitors alike. In recent years, the idea of Istanbul's secret tunnels has found new life in popular culture. Turkish television dramas set in the Ottoman era often feature scenes of characters navigating torch-lit underground passages. Video games set in the city invariably include levels where players explore subterranean mazes. There's even been talk of developing a "tunnel tour" for tourists, though concerns about safety and preservation have so far prevented this from becoming a reality.

The enduring appeal of the tunnel legends speaks to something deeper than mere historical curiosity. In a city as ancient and layered as Istanbul, where the past is always palpable, the idea of a hidden world just beneath our feet is powerfully alluring. The tunnels represent mystery, adventure, and the tantalizing possibility that there are still secrets waiting to be uncovered in this most historic of cities.

Moreover, the tunnel stories reflect Istanbul's unique position as a crossroads of cultures and continents. The idea of secret passages linking Europe and Asia, connecting mosques and churches, palaces and markets, speaks to the city's long history as a place where different worlds meet and mingle.

For the people of Istanbul, the legends of the underground tunnels are more than just entertaining stories. They're a way of connecting with the city's long and complex history. Every time a new construction project unearths some ancient structure, or a homeowner discovers an old cellar that extends further than expected, the tunnel legends gain new life. People wonder: could this be an entrance to the fabled network? What secrets might lie just beyond that bricked-up doorway?

In a way, the persistence of these legends in the face of skepticism and lack of concrete evidence is itself a testament to the enduring magic of Istanbul. This is a city where the line between myth and reality has always been blurred, where the fantastical and the everyday coexist in a unique harmony.

As night falls over Istanbul and the call to prayer echoes from ancient minarets, it's easy to imagine that somewhere beneath the streets, hidden from the eyes of the modern world, the old tunnels still wind their way through the earth. Perhaps in some forgotten chamber, the ghosts of emperors and sultans still hold court. Maybe in a dusty passage, undisturbed for centuries, some long-lost treasure still waits to be discovered.

· · ·

And who knows? Perhaps one day, a construction worker's pickaxe or an archaeologist's careful brush will reveal the entrance to a passage that proves the legends true. Until then, the underground tunnels of Istanbul remain one of the city's most intriguing mysteries, a story whispered in cafes and bazaars, a secret waiting to be uncovered beneath the feet of millions.

24

THE BLESSED PIGEONS

T he Eyüp Sultan Mosque stands serene on the shores of the Golden Horn, its minarets reaching skyward, a beacon of faith and history. But it's not just the architecture or the sacred relics within that draw visitors from across Istanbul and beyond. It's also the pigeons - hundreds of them, cooing and fluttering around the courtyard, seemingly as much a part of the mosque as its stone walls and ornate tiles.

. . .

These aren't just any pigeons. According to a cherished legend, they are the descendants of a pair of birds that played a crucial role in Islamic history, helping to protect the Prophet Muhammad in his hour of need. This tale, passed down through generations, has elevated these humble city birds to a status approaching the sacred.

The story begins in 7th century Arabia, long before the founding of Istanbul or the construction of the Eyüp Sultan Mosque. It was a time of great upheaval, as the new religion of Islam began to spread, challenging the established order. The Prophet Muhammad, facing persecution in his hometown of Mecca, was forced to flee with his closest companion, Abu Bakr.

As the legend goes, Muhammad and Abu Bakr sought refuge in a cave on Mount Thawr, just outside Mecca. Their pursuers, intent on capturing or killing the Prophet, were close behind. It seemed only a matter of time before they were discovered.

But then, a miracle occurred. As Muhammad and Abu Bakr huddled in the cave, a pair of pigeons appeared. Guided by divine inspiration, the birds quickly built a nest at the entrance of the cave. Then, completing the disguise, a spider spun an intricate web across the cave's mouth.

When the pursuers arrived, they saw the undisturbed spider's web and the nesting pigeons. Reasoning that no one could have entered the cave without breaking the web and disturbing the birds, they moved on, never realizing how close they had come to their quarry. Thanks to the pigeons and the spider, the Prophet was saved, free to continue his journey and spread his message.

This pivotal moment in Islamic history, known as the Hijra, marks the beginning of the Islamic calendar. And while the cave on Mount Thawr is far from Istanbul, the legend of the protective pigeons found new life centuries later at the Eyüp Sultan Mosque.

The mosque itself has a storied history. It was built in the 15th century, shortly after the Ottoman conquest of Constantinople, on the site where Abu Ayyub al-Ansari, a close companion of the Prophet Muhammad, is said to have been buried. Abu Ayyub had participated in the first Arab siege of Constantinople in the 7th century, dying outside the city walls. His tomb, rediscovered centuries later, became a place of pilgrimage.

As the legend of the blessed pigeons spread, it became entwined with the sanctity of the Eyüp Sultan Mosque. People began to see the flocks of pigeons that naturally gathered in the mosque's courtyard as the descendants of those original birds that had protected the Prophet. Over time, caring for these pigeons became seen as a form of religious devotion, a way of honoring both the Prophet's legacy and the memory of Abu Ayyub al-Ansari.

The belief in the blessed nature of these pigeons has led to some unique customs at the Eyüp Sultan Mosque. Visitors often bring bags of seeds or breadcrumbs to feed the birds, seeing it as a way to gain blessings or have their prayers answered. Some even believe that if a pigeon lands on your shoulder, it's a sign of particularly good fortune.

. . .

The mosque's caretakers have embraced this tradition, setting up dedicated feeding areas and water troughs for the pigeons. They also ensure that the birds have safe nesting spots in the nooks and crannies of the mosque's architecture. This care has resulted in a large and healthy pigeon population, further reinforcing the legend of their blessed status.

But the story of the Eyüp Sultan pigeons is more than just a quaint local custom. It speaks to deeper themes in Islamic thought and Turkish culture. The idea of animals serving a divine purpose, of the natural world being in harmony with spiritual truths, is a recurring motif in Islamic tradition. The legend of the pigeons reinforces the belief in a cosmos where every creature, no matter how small, can play a role in the grand design.

Moreover, the tale reflects the Turkish people's long-standing affinity for birds, particularly pigeons. Throughout Ottoman history, pigeon-keeping was a popular pastime, with elaborate dovecotes being a common feature in the courtyards of mosques and private homes. Pigeons were valued not just for their beauty and the sport of pigeon racing, but also for their practical uses in carrying messages and providing fertilizer.

This cultural appreciation for pigeons merged seamlessly with the religious legend at Eyüp Sultan, creating a unique synthesis of faith and tradition. The blessed pigeons became a symbol of Istanbul itself - a city where the spiritual and the everyday often intersect in unexpected ways.

As with many legends, the story of the Eyüp Sultan pigeons has evolved over time. Some versions claim that the original blessed pigeons flew all the way from Arabia to Istanbul, guided by divine will to make their home at the mosque. Others suggest that Abu Ayyub al-Ansari himself brought a pair of the Prophet's pigeons with him on his campaign to Constantinople, and that the current flock are their descendants.

These embellishments, while historically unlikely, speak to the way living legends grow and change to reflect the needs and beliefs of each generation. For the people of Istanbul, the pigeons of Eyüp Sultan have become more than just birds - they're a living link to a revered past, a daily reminder of the miraculous in the midst of the mundane.

The legend has also had some unexpected real-world impacts. The protected status of the Eyüp Sultan pigeons has made the mosque a de facto bird sanctuary in the heart of bustling Istanbul. This has attracted the attention of conservationists and bird lovers, who see the site as an important urban habitat for pigeons and other bird species.

Some scientists have even studied the Eyüp Sultan pigeon population, curious about how these birds might differ from other urban pigeon populations due to centuries of protected status and careful breeding. While no miraculous differences have been found, the studies have provided valuable data on urban wildlife adaptation.

The blessed pigeons have also become a draw for tourists, both Muslim and non-Muslim alike. Many visitors to Istanbul make a point of stopping at Eyüp Sultan Mosque, not just to admire its architecture or pay respects at Abu Ayyub's tomb, but also to experience the unique atmosphere created by the swirling flocks of pigeons. The sight of hundreds of birds taking flight at once, their wings catching the light as they circle the minarets, has become an iconic Istanbul image.

For many, feeding the pigeons at Eyüp Sultan has become a form of participatory folklore - a way to connect with centuries of tradition and perhaps, just perhaps, receive a touch of divine blessing. Children especially delight in tossing seeds to the birds, their laughter mingling with the cooing of the pigeons and the call to prayer.

Of course, as with any intersection of wildlife and human activity, there have been challenges. The large number of pigeons can sometimes create cleanliness issues for the mosque. The caretakers work hard to maintain a balance between honoring the legend and preserving the sanctity and cleanliness of the religious site.

Some wildlife experts have also raised concerns about the practice of feeding wild birds, arguing that it can lead to overpopulation and dependency. These modern considerations have led to ongoing discussions about how best to honor the legend while also being responsible stewards of both the mosque and the urban ecosystem.

Yet despite these practical concerns, the legend of the blessed pigeons continues to thrive. In a rapidly modernizing Istanbul, where skyscrapers rise next to centuries-old mosques and where ancient traditions often clash with contemporary life, the pigeons of Eyüp Sultan offer a moment of constancy, a living link to a storied past.

. . .

As the sun sets over the Golden Horn and the last rays of light glint off the mosque's domes, the pigeons of Eyüp Sultan settle in for the night. In the gathering dusk, it's easy to imagine that among them might be descendants of those original birds, still watching over the faithful, still embodying a miracle that spans centuries and continents.

For the people of Istanbul, whether they fully believe the legend or not, these pigeons represent something special - a everyday reminder of the extraordinary, a flutter of the divine in the heart of the city. In their gentle cooing and graceful flight, the blessed pigeons of Eyüp Sultan continue to weave together strands of history, faith, and urban life, creating a uniquely Istanbul story that shows no sign of fading away.

25

THE MOVING OBELISK

In the heart of Istanbul's historic Sultanahmet district, stands a monument that has puzzled and fascinated locals and visitors for centuries. The Obelisk of Theodosius, a towering ancient Egyptian monolith, has been a silent witness to the city's tumultuous history since its arrival in Constantinople in 390 AD. But it's not just its age or origin that captures the imagination - it's the persistent legend that the obelisk is slowly sinking into the ground, defying both gravity and logic.

. . .

The obelisk itself is a marvel of ancient engineering. Originally carved from a single piece of red granite during the reign of Thutmose III in the 15th century BC, it once stood proudly in the Temple of Karnak in Luxor, Egypt. Nearly two thousand years later, Roman Emperor Theodosius I had it transported to what was then Constantinople to adorn the spina of the Hippodrome, the city's grand arena for chariot races and public spectacles.

Standing at 19.6 meters tall (about 64 feet), the obelisk is covered in hieroglyphs celebrating the victories of Thutmose III. Its pointed top, once capped with gleaming bronze, reaches towards the sky like a stone finger. The base, adorned with reliefs depicting Theodosius I and his family watching the games in the Hippodrome, tells a story of imperial power and ambition.

But it's what's supposedly happening beneath the surface that has sparked centuries of speculation and debate. According to local legend, the Obelisk of Theodosius is slowly but steadily sinking into the ground. Some claim it descends by as much as 2-3 centimeters each year, while others insist the movement is more subtle, perhaps only a few millimeters.

The origins of this belief are lost to time, but it has been a part of Istanbul's folklore for generations. Old-timers in the city swear that the obelisk stood much taller in their youth, pointing to various marks on the stone as evidence of its descent. Tour guides often include the tale in their narratives, adding an air of mystery to the ancient monument.

One popular version of the legend claims that when the obelisk finally sinks completely into the ground, it will mark the end of the world - or at least, the end of Istanbul. This apocalyptic twist adds a sense of urgency to the tale, turning a simple architectural curiosity into a portent of doom.

Another strand of the story suggests that the sinking is not a natural phenomenon but the result of an ancient curse. According to this version, when the obelisk was removed from its original home in Egypt, the priests of Karnak placed a hex on it, condemning it to forever seek its native soil. This curse, some say, is what drives the obelisk ever downward, as it tries to return to the land of the pharaohs.

The idea of the moving obelisk has spawned numerous urban legends and local customs. Some Istanbulites make it a yearly tradition to visit the monument and measure its height, convinced they'll be able to track its descent. Others claim that if you press your ear to the base of the obelisk on a quiet night, you can hear the faint grinding of stone against stone as it sinks.

Over the years, various explanations have been proposed for the obelisk's supposed movement. Some point to Istanbul's long history of earthquakes, suggesting that seismic activity might be gradually driving the monument into the ground. Others blame the city's notoriously unstable soil, which has caused problems for buildings and infrastructure throughout Istanbul's history.

A more poetic theory posits that the obelisk is sinking under the weight of the history it has witnessed. From the glory days of the Byzantine Empire to the Ottoman conquest, from the fall of sultans to the rise of the modern Turkish republic, the obelisk has stood through it all. Perhaps, some say, it's simply tired and ready to rest.

. . .

Of course, scientists and historians take a more skeptical view of
the legend. Careful measurements and studies have found no
evidence of significant movement in the obelisk. Experts point out
that if the monument were indeed sinking at the rate claimed in
some versions of the legend, it would have disappeared entirely
centuries ago.

Archaeologists have also noted that the obelisk's base is actually
higher than the original ground level of the Hippodrome. Over the
centuries, the accumulation of debris and the raising of the
surrounding area have, if anything, made the obelisk appear
shorter relative to its surroundings, rather than the obelisk itself
sinking.

Yet despite the lack of scientific evidence, the legend persists. It
has become part of the cultural fabric of Istanbul, a story that
reflects the city's complex relationship with its multi-layered
history. The idea of an ancient Egyptian monument, brought to
the city by Roman emperors, potentially sinking into Turkish soil
seems to encapsulate Istanbul's unique position as a crossroads of
civilizations.

The tale of the moving obelisk has also found its way into popular
culture. Local artists have created works inspired by the legend,
imagining what the city might look like when only the tip of the
obelisk remains visible. Writers have used the story as a metaphor
for Istanbul's constant state of change, with the past slowly sinking
away as the modern city rises around it.

. . .

In recent years, the legend has taken on new life in the digital age. Social media is often abuzz with posts from visitors claiming to have proof of the obelisk's movement. Doctored photos showing the monument at impossible angles or heights circulate regularly, fueling further speculation and debate.

The story has even inspired some amateur archaeologists to propose excavations around the base of the obelisk to settle the matter once and for all. However, given the historical significance of the site and the potential risks to the monument, such proposals have been firmly rejected by authorities.

For the millions of tourists who visit Sultanahmet Square each year, the legend of the moving obelisk adds an extra layer of intrigue to an already impressive sight. Many can be seen scrutinizing the base of the monument, looking for signs of sinking or trying to gauge its height against nearby buildings.

But beyond its appeal to visitors, the tale of the Obelisk of Theodosius speaks to something deeper in the psyche of Istanbul. In a city where the ground has literally shifted over centuries of earthquakes and rebuilding, where empires have risen and fallen, the idea of a seemingly immovable object slowly descending into the earth resonates on a profound level.

It's a reminder of the impermanence of all things, even those made of solid granite. It speaks to the way the past is always present in Istanbul, but also always changing, sinking beneath the surface only to be rediscovered in new ways.

· · ·

The legend also reflects the Turkish people's complex relationship with the many layers of history beneath their feet. The obelisk, like so many monuments in Istanbul, is a remnant of past empires and civilizations. Its supposed movement could be seen as a metaphor for the way these historical legacies are constantly being reinterpreted and reimagined in the context of modern Turkey.

As night falls over Sultanahmet Square and the obelisk is illuminated against the darkening sky, it's easy to understand why the legend has endured for so long. There's something almost magical about the monument's presence, a sense of ancient mysteries and untold stories.

Whether the Obelisk of Theodosius is truly sinking or not, its legend has become an integral part of Istanbul's cultural land-scape. It's a story that bridges the gap between the city's ancient past and its vibrant present, a tale that continues to evolve with each retelling.

In the end, perhaps the truth of the obelisk's movement (or lack thereof) is less important than what the legend represents. It's a testament to Istanbul's enduring ability to blend fact and fiction, history and myth, into narratives that capture the imagination and stand the test of time.

As the city continues to grow and change around it, the Obelisk of Theodosius remains a constant presence, a silent sentinel that holds its secrets close. And who knows? Perhaps centuries from now, long after our current debates have been forgotten, someone will look at the obelisk and swear that it stands just a little shorter than it used to, keeping the legend alive for generations to come.

26

THE SECRET OF LEANDER'S TOWER

On a tiny islet in the Bosphorus Strait, a stone's throw from the Asian shore of Istanbul, stands a structure that has captured imaginations for centuries. The Maiden's Tower, or Kız Kulesi in Turkish, rises from the waters like a sentinel, its white walls and red-coned roof a familiar sight to anyone traveling between Europe and Asia. But behind its picturesque facade lies a tale of love, tragedy, and the enduring power of myth.

. . .

The story of Leander's Tower, as it's also known, begins not in Istanbul, but in the ancient Greek city of Sestos, on the European side of the Hellespont (now called the Dardanelles). There lived a priestess of Aphrodite named Hero, whose beauty was said to rival that of the goddess she served. On the opposite shore, in the city of Abydos, lived a young man named Leander.

During a festival of Aphrodite, Leander crossed the strait to Sestos and encountered Hero. It was love at first sight, a passion so intense that it seemed to set the very air around them aflame. But their love was forbidden. As a priestess, Hero had taken vows of chastity, and the treacherous waters of the Hellespont separated their homes.

Undeterred by these obstacles, the lovers devised a plan. Each night, Hero would light a lamp in her tower, and Leander would swim across the strait, guided by this beacon of love. Under cover of darkness, they would spend precious hours together before Leander had to return home before dawn.

Night after night, through calm seas and storms, Leander made the perilous journey, strengthened by his love for Hero. And each night, Hero would anxiously watch the waters, her heart only easing when she saw Leander's head break the surface.

But fate, it seemed, was not content to let their love story unfold untroubled. One autumn night, a fierce storm blew in from the Aegean. The winds howled, whipping the sea into a frenzy of white-capped waves. Hero, worried for her lover but unwilling to break their pact, lit her lamp as always.

· · ·

Leander, seeing the light, plunged into the roiling waters. But the storm was too strong. Wave after wave crashed over him, and the wind kept blowing out Hero's lamp. Disoriented and exhausted, Leander was swept away by the current. As dawn broke, the waters calmed, and Hero saw Leander's lifeless body washed up on the rocks below her tower.

Overcome with grief, Hero threw herself from the tower to join her lover in death. The tale of their tragic love spread throughout the ancient world, immortalized by poets and storytellers.

As centuries passed and empires rose and fell, the story of Hero and Leander became intertwined with the Maiden's Tower in the Bosphorus. Though the original tale was set further south, the isolated tower in Istanbul captured the imaginations of locals and visitors alike. It became common to hear tour guides and locals refer to the structure as "Leander's Tower," recounting the ancient Greek myth as if it had happened right there in the Bosphorus.

The real history of the Maiden's Tower is almost as colorful as the myth. The first structure on the islet was built in 408 BCE by an Athenian general, who used it to control shipping and collect tolls. Over the centuries, it was rebuilt and repurposed many times. The Byzantines used it as a watchtower and built a chain across the strait to control passage. Later, the Ottomans turned it into a lighthouse and quarantine station.

But it's the legends that have truly kept the Maiden's Tower alive in the public imagination. In addition to the tale of Hero and Leander, there's a popular Turkish legend about a sultan who, upon hearing a prophecy that his daughter would die from a snakebite on her 18th birthday, built the tower to protect her. Despite his efforts, a snake hidden in a basket of fruit bit the princess, fulfilling the prophecy.

These stories, blending and evolving over time, have given the Maiden's Tower a mystical aura. On misty mornings, when the tower seems to float above the water, it's easy to imagine Hero standing at the window, scanning the waves for her lover. At night, with the tower illuminated against the dark waters, one can almost see the flickering of her lamp, still guiding lost souls across the strait.

The tower has become a symbol of Istanbul itself, a bridge between myth and history, Europe and Asia, land and sea. It features prominently in literature, art, and film, each new interpretation adding another layer to its rich mythology.

In the 19th century, the tower caught the eye of Russian painter Ivan Aivazovsky, who created several romantic depictions of it bathed in moonlight or surrounded by stormy seas. These paintings helped popularize the tower's image internationally, cementing its place in the popular imagination as a site of mystery and romance.

The 20th century brought new chapters to the tower's story. During the Cold War, it was rumored to house secret listening devices, monitoring communications between Soviet submarines in the Black Sea. In the 1990s, it was restored and opened to the public as a restaurant and tourist attraction, allowing visitors to step inside the legend for the first time.

.   .   .

Today, boats ferry tourists to and from the tower, where they can climb the winding stairs to the top for panoramic views of Istanbul. The interior houses a small museum detailing the tower's history and legends. In the evenings, the tower is lit up, its reflection shimmering on the waters of the Bosphorus.

But even with its modern amenities and steady stream of visitors, the Maiden's Tower retains an air of mystery. Many who visit report a strange sense of deja vu, as if they've seen the tower in a dream. Others swear they've heard whispers on the wind, or caught glimpses of shadowy figures in the windows.

Local fishermen tell stories of lights seen moving in the tower late at night, long after the last ferry has departed. Some claim to have heard a woman's voice singing a mournful tune, the sound carrying across the water on still nights. Skeptics dismiss these tales as the product of overactive imaginations or clever marketing, but believers insist there's more to the Maiden's Tower than meets the eye.

The tower has also become a popular spot for marriage proposals, with couples drawn by its romantic associations. It's said that a promise of love made at the tower will last forever, blessed by the spirits of Hero and Leander. Whether one believes in such things or not, there's no denying the romantic atmosphere as the sun sets behind the Istanbul skyline, painting the waters of the Bosphorus in shades of gold and crimson.

In a city as ancient and storied as Istanbul, where every stone seems to hold a secret, the Maiden's Tower stands out as a place where the line between history and legend blurs. It serves as a reminder that some stories are too powerful to be confined by the boundaries of time or geography.

The tale of Hero and Leander, transplanted from the Hellespont to the Bosphorus, speaks to universal themes of love, sacrifice, and the human desire to overcome seemingly insurmountable obstacles. In a world that often feels divided, the image of Leander swimming across the strait, guided by Hero's unwavering light, resonates with anyone who has ever been separated from a loved one.

As night falls over Istanbul and the lights of the city twinkle to life, the Maiden's Tower shines like a beacon in the darkness. And who's to say that, on some nights, when the moon is full and the waters are calm, the spirits of two ancient lovers don't still meet there, defying death as they once defied distance, their love story playing out for eternity in the shadow of the tower that bears their legend.

In the end, perhaps it doesn't matter whether the events of the myth actually took place at this specific location. The power of the Maiden's Tower lies in its ability to connect us to something larger than ourselves, to remind us of the enduring nature of love and the stories we tell about it. As long as there are lovers in the world, as long as there are those willing to risk everything for a chance at happiness, the legend of Leander's Tower will continue to captivate and inspire.

THE TALE OF THE IMMORTAL JEW

There's a tale that has been whispered for centuries. It's a story that bridges cultures and religions, linking the ancient streets of Jerusalem to the bustling bazaars of the Bosphorus. This is the legend of the Immortal Jew, also known as the Wandering Jew, whose path of eternal exile is said to sometimes lead him through the heart of Istanbul.

. . .

The story begins in Jerusalem, nearly two thousand years ago, on the day of Jesus Christ's crucifixion. As Jesus stumbled under the weight of his cross on the way to Golgotha, he paused before a shoemaker's shop, seeking a moment's rest. The shoemaker, a man named Ahasuerus, was busy with his work and annoyed by the commotion outside. When Jesus leaned against his doorway, Ahasuerus harshly drove him away, shouting, "Go on! Move faster!"

Jesus, looking at the shoemaker with both sorrow and divine authority, is said to have replied, "I go, but you will walk until I come again." With these words, Ahasuerus was cursed to wander the earth, never aging, never finding rest, until the Second Coming of Christ.

And so began the shoemaker's eternal journey. He walked out of Jerusalem that very day, leaving behind his shop, his family, and everything he had known. As years turned to decades, and decades to centuries, Ahasuerus roamed the world, witnessing the rise and fall of empires, the birth of new religions, and the ever-changing face of humanity.

It was perhaps inevitable that his wanderings would eventually bring him to Istanbul, a city that has long stood at the crossroads of civilizations. The first reported sighting of Ahasuerus in the city dates back to the Byzantine era, when Constantinople was still the capital of the Eastern Roman Empire. A monk claimed to have encountered a strange, ageless man near the Great Palace, who spoke of events from centuries past as if he had witnessed them firsthand.

· · ·

As the centuries passed and Constantinople fell to the Ottomans, becoming Istanbul, the legend of the Immortal Jew took root in the city's rich soil of myths and legends. The story resonated with the diverse population of Istanbul, a place where Christians, Muslims, and Jews had long lived side by side, each bringing their own traditions and beliefs to the cultural mosaic of the city.

In the narrow streets of Balat, the old Jewish quarter, older residents still speak of encounters with a mysterious stranger who appears out of nowhere, often during times of trouble or significant change. They describe a man with ancient eyes, wearing clothes that seem out of place in any era, who speaks perfect Turkish tinged with an accent no one can quite place.

One popular version of the legend claims that Ahasuerus appears in Istanbul once every hundred years, drawn by the city's unique position as a bridge between East and West. Some say he comes to atone for his sin, helping those in need as a way to make amends for his treatment of Jesus. Others believe he is drawn by the city's own long history, finding a kinship in a place that, like him, has witnessed the turning of ages.

The sightings of Ahasuerus in Istanbul often coincide with moments of historical significance. There are tales of him walking among the ruins after the great fire of 1660, comforting those who had lost everything. During the turbulent years of World War I, when the Ottoman Empire was crumbling, some claimed to have seen him near the Sublime Porte, shaking his head sadly as if he had seen such falls before.

In the early days of the Turkish Republic, as Istanbul grappled with rapid modernization, there were reports of an ageless man in the Grand Bazaar, marveling at the changes while reminiscing about the days of Justinian and Suleiman the Magnificent as if they were recent memories.

The legend has taken on different meanings for different communities within Istanbul. For the city's Jewish population, long accustomed to diaspora and persecution, the tale of Ahasuerus carries a particular resonance. Some see him as a symbol of Jewish resilience and survival against all odds. Others view his eternal wandering as a cautionary tale about the consequences of turning away from compassion and faith.

Among Istanbul's Christians, the story is often told as a reminder of the importance of kindness and the heavy price of cruelty. It's not uncommon to hear parents admonishing their children to be helpful and hospitable, lest they end up like the shoemaker who turned away Christ.

For many of Istanbul's Muslims, the legend of the Immortal Jew has been incorporated into Islamic eschatology. Some believe that Ahasuerus's wanderings will only end with the return of Jesus, who is recognized as a prophet in Islam. His appearances in the city are seen by some as signs of impending significant events or spiritual awakenings.

The tale has also found its way into Istanbul's rich literary tradition. Poets and storytellers have long been inspired by the figure of the eternal wanderer, using him as a metaphor for the city itself - ancient, ever-changing, a witness to the sweep of history. In the coffee houses of Beyoğlu, where intellectuals gather to discuss philosophy and politics, the story of Ahasuerus is sometimes invoked in debates about the nature of time, punishment, and redemption.

One of the most intriguing aspects of the Immortal Jew legend in Istanbul is how it has evolved to reflect the city's changing face. In recent years, as Istanbul has grown into a modern metropolis, there have been reported sightings of Ahasuerus in unexpected places. Some claim to have seen him riding the metro, an ancient man bewildered by the speed and technology of the modern world. Others swear they've spotted him in the business districts, his timeless eyes filled with both wonder and sorrow at the towering skyscrapers.

These modern incarnations of the legend often carry a note of environmental or social commentary. In a time of rapid urban development and growing concerns about sustainability, the Immortal Jew is sometimes depicted as a voice of warning, a witness to the long-term consequences of human actions.

Despite the fantastical nature of the tale, the legend of the Immortal Jew continues to captivate the imagination of Istanbul's residents and visitors alike. Walking tours of the old city often include stops at places where Ahasuerus is said to have been sighted. Some local artisans even create souvenirs inspired by the legend - amulets that supposedly protect the wearer from curses, or intricate miniature paintings depicting scenes from the Wandering Jew's eternal journey.

Skeptics, of course, dismiss the story as nothing more than folklore, a myth born from the blending of different religious and cultural traditions in Istanbul's melting pot. They point out the logical impossibilities of the tale and the lack of any concrete evidence for the existence of an immortal wanderer.

Yet even for those who don't believe in the literal truth of the legend, the story of Ahasuerus holds a powerful allure. It speaks to universal themes of guilt and redemption, of the weight of history and the search for meaning in a changing world. In a city like Istanbul, where the past is always present and where different cultures and beliefs have intermingled for centuries, such a tale finds fertile ground.

As night falls over Istanbul and the call to prayer echoes from ancient minarets, it's easy to imagine Ahasuerus walking the city's streets. Perhaps he pauses on the Galata Bridge, looking out over the Golden Horn, remembering when it was just a narrow inlet filled with fishing boats. Maybe he wanders through the Grand Bazaar, recalling when it was first built, marveling at how some things change while others remain eternally the same.

The legend of the Immortal Jew serves as a reminder that Istanbul is a city where the boundaries between past and present, myth and reality, are often blurred. It's a place where an ancient curse from Jerusalem can find new life in the stories told in Turkish coffee houses, where a wanderer from two millennia ago might still find himself at home in the eternal city on the Bosphorus.

Whether seen as a literal figure or a powerful metaphor, the Immortal Jew of Istanbul embodies the city's enduring ability to absorb and reinterpret the stories of many cultures. In the tale of Ahasuerus, we find echoes of Istanbul's own journey through time - a witness to the ages, forever changing yet somehow always the same, carrying the weight of history while constantly moving forward into the future.

As long as there are streets to wander in Istanbul, as long as there are stories to be told and retold, the legend of the Immortal Jew will likely persist. It will continue to evolve, adapting to new eras and new concerns, but always remaining at its core a tale of endurance, of the long arc of history, and of the complex interplay between punishment and redemption that speaks to something deep in the human spirit.

28

THE LOST MOSAIC

The Hagia Sophia, with its soaring dome and centuries of history, holds many secrets. But perhaps none is as tantalizing as the rumor of a hidden mosaic, a masterpiece of Byzantine art said to be concealed behind layers of plaster and paint. This legend, whispered in the shadowy corners of Istanbul's old city, speaks of a work so magnificent, so controversial, that it was covered up during the Ottoman conversion of the great church into a mosque.

. . .

The story begins in the 6th century, when Emperor Justinian I ordered the construction of Hagia Sophia. The building was to be a testament to the glory of God and the power of the Byzantine Empire. No expense was spared in its decoration, with marble from across the empire and mosaics that gleamed with gold and precious stones.

Among these mosaics, according to the legend, was one of unparalleled size and beauty. Some versions of the tale claim it depicted Christ in Majesty, seated on a rainbow throne and surrounded by angels. Others speak of a complex scene showing the Last Judgment, with the saved ascending to heaven and the damned cast into hell. Still others insist it was a representation of the Virgin Mary, her arms outstretched in blessing over the city of Constantinople.

Whatever its subject, the mosaic was said to cover an entire wall of the church, possibly in the upper galleries where the empress and her court would worship. Its size and prominent placement made it a focal point for all who entered Hagia Sophia, a glittering testament to the skill of Byzantine artisans and the depth of Christian faith.

For nearly a thousand years, this mosaic (if it indeed existed) watched over the great church, witnessing coronations, excommunications, and the ebb and flow of empire. But in 1453, everything changed. Constantinople fell to the Ottoman Turks, and Hagia Sophia was converted into a mosque.

The new rulers of the city, adhering to Islamic prohibitions against representational art in places of worship, faced a dilemma. The Christian mosaics that adorned Hagia Sophia were masterpieces, but they were also deeply inappropriate for a mosque. Some were destroyed, others were plastered over. But the fate of the great mosaic remains a mystery.

According to the legend, Sultan Mehmed the Conqueror, impressed by the beauty and craftsmanship of the mosaic, ordered it to be preserved. Rather than destroy it, he commanded that it be carefully covered, hidden from view but protected for future generations. Some versions of the story claim that the sultan believed that one day, the mosaic would be revealed again, perhaps when the world was ready for the message it contained.

Over the centuries, as Hagia Sophia served as the principal mosque of Istanbul, the memory of the hidden mosaic faded into legend. But it was never entirely forgotten. Rumors persisted, passed down through generations of Istanbul's residents. Some claimed that on quiet nights, when the great building was empty, one could hear the faint tinkling of mosaic tiles shifting behind the plaster, as if the hidden masterpiece was trying to break free.

The legend gained new life in the 19th century, as the Ottoman Empire began to open up to Western influence. European travelers and scholars, fascinated by the history of Hagia Sophia, began to investigate the rumors of the hidden mosaic. Some even claimed to have seen evidence of its existence - a glint of gold visible through a crack in the plaster, or the faint outline of a face visible under certain lighting conditions.

These rumors reached a fever pitch in the early 20th century, as Hagia Sophia underwent a series of restorations. In 1931, a team led by Thomas Whittemore began the painstaking work of uncovering the building's Byzantine mosaics. As plaster was carefully removed, revealing glittering scenes of angels and emperors, hopes ran high that the legendary great mosaic would finally be rediscovered.

But despite years of work, no trace of the massive, wall-spanning mosaic was found. This lack of physical evidence did little to dampen enthusiasm for the legend, however. If anything, it added to the mystery. Theories abounded as to why the mosaic remained hidden. Some suggested that it was concealed behind a false wall, others that it had been carefully removed tile by tile and hidden in a secret chamber somewhere in the vast building.

The conversion of Hagia Sophia into a museum in 1935 opened up new possibilities for exploration. For decades, researchers combed through the building, using increasingly sophisticated technology in their search for the lost mosaic. Ground-penetrating radar, infrared cameras, and other cutting-edge tools were employed, but still, the great mosaic remained elusive.

In recent years, as Hagia Sophia has once again been converted into a mosque, the legend of the hidden mosaic has taken on new significance. For some, it represents a lost piece of Christian heritage, a masterpiece of Byzantine art waiting to be rediscovered. For others, it's a symbol of the building's complex history, a reminder of the layers of culture and faith that have shaped Istanbul over the centuries.

The persistent belief in the hidden mosaic speaks to something deeper than mere archaeological curiosity. It reflects humanity's enduring fascination with lost treasures and hidden knowledge. The idea that a masterpiece could be concealed for centuries, waiting for the right moment to be revealed, captures the imagination in a powerful way.

Moreover, the legend of the hidden mosaic serves as a metaphor for Hagia Sophia itself - a building that has been many things to many people over its long history. Like the purported mosaic, hidden beneath layers of plaster and paint, the true nature of Hagia Sophia seems to shift depending on who's looking at it and from what angle.

The story has inspired countless works of fiction, from novels to films, each offering their own interpretation of what the hidden mosaic might depict and what its discovery could mean. Some portray it as a religious artifact of immense spiritual power, others as a key to unlocking historical or mystical secrets.

In Istanbul's bustling bazaars and quiet teahouses, the legend continues to be debated and embellished. Some locals claim to have relatives who worked on Hagia Sophia's restorations and saw evidence of the mosaic. Others insist that the secret of its location is known only to a select few, passed down through generations of guardians.

Tourists visiting Hagia Sophia often ask guides about the hidden mosaic, eager for any hint of its existence. Some even claim to feel a special energy in certain parts of the building, convinced they're standing near the concealed masterpiece. This blend of history, myth, and spiritual longing is quintessentially Istanbul, a city where the line between fact and legend is often blurred.

· · ·

The legend has also had some unexpected real-world impacts. It has inspired renewed interest in Byzantine art and history, leading to funding for research and conservation efforts. The search for the hidden mosaic has led to the discovery of other, smaller mosaics and frescoes that had been overlooked or forgotten.

For archaeologists and historians, the legend of the hidden mosaic presents both a tantalizing possibility and a frustrating enigma. While most experts are skeptical about the existence of a massive, undiscovered mosaic, they acknowledge that Hagia Sophia still holds many secrets. The building's vast size, complex history, and numerous modifications over the centuries mean that there's always the possibility of new discoveries.

Some scholars have proposed alternative theories to explain the origins of the legend. Perhaps, they suggest, the story conflates several different mosaics that once existed in Hagia Sophia. Or maybe it's a cultural memory of the building's Great Entrance mosaic, which was visible until the 18th century before being plastered over.

Regardless of its origins or veracity, the legend of the hidden mosaic has become an integral part of Hagia Sophia's mystique. It adds an element of mystery and possibility to a building already steeped in history and spiritual significance. For many visitors, the idea that there might be an undiscovered masterpiece just out of sight makes their experience of Hagia Sophia even more profound.

As debates continue about Hagia Sophia's status and use, the legend of the hidden mosaic serves as a reminder of the building's complex legacy. It's a story that encompasses Christianity and

Islam, art and faith, preservation and change. In many ways, it encapsulates the essence of Istanbul itself - a city where the past is always present, where ancient mysteries coexist with modern life.

Whether the great mosaic exists or not, the search for it has already yielded valuable results. It has sparked conversations about history, art, and cultural heritage. It has inspired people to look at Hagia Sophia with fresh eyes, to consider what other secrets the ancient building might hold.

As night falls over Istanbul and Hagia Sophia's silhouette dominates the skyline, it's easy to imagine the hidden mosaic waiting in the darkness, its golden tiles catching the faint light of the moon. Perhaps one day it will be uncovered, revealing its long-hidden splendor to the world. Or perhaps it will remain forever concealed, a tantalizing mystery that continues to capture imaginations for generations to come. Either way, the legend of the hidden mosaic will likely endure, a shimmering thread in the intricate tapestry of stories that make up the history of Hagia Sophia and Istanbul itself.

29

THE WEEPING TREE OF GÜLHANE PARK

In the heart of Gülhane Park, stands a tree unlike any other. To the casual observer, it might seem unremarkable - an old plane tree, its branches reaching towards the sky, its leaves rustling in the Bosphorus breeze. But as night falls and the park empties of picnickers and tourists, this tree is said to come alive in a most unusual way. For according to local legend, this is the Weeping Tree of Gülhane, a living relic that sheds tears for the lost glory of the Ottoman Empire.

· · ·

The story of the Weeping Tree begins in the late 19th century, during the twilight years of Ottoman rule. Gülhane Park, which had once been part of the outer gardens of Topkapi Palace, was opened to the public in 1912. It was a time of great change and uncertainty for the empire, as modernization efforts clashed with centuries-old traditions and external pressures mounted from all sides.

Among the many trees planted in the park during this period was a young plane tree, unremarkable at first glance. But as the years passed and the Ottoman Empire faced increasing challenges, people began to notice something strange about this particular tree. Groundskeepers reported finding the area around its trunk inexplicably damp in the mornings, even on days when there had been no rain. Some claimed to have seen droplets of moisture forming on its leaves and branches in the dead of night, glistening in the moonlight like tears.

At first, these occurrences were dismissed as natural phenomena - perhaps an unusually high water table or a quirk of the tree's physiology. But as the Ottoman Empire entered its final years, the stories surrounding the tree took on a more mystical character.

It was a night watchman who first connected the tree's weeping to the empire's decline. He claimed to have heard soft, mournful sounds coming from the tree late one night, coinciding with news of a particularly devastating military defeat. From that point on, people began to see the tree as a kind of living barometer for the empire's fortunes, its tears flowing more freely with each setback and loss.

. . .

The legend grew stronger in 1922, when the last Ottoman Sultan, Mehmed VI, was deposed and sent into exile. Eyewitnesses swore that on the night of his departure, the Weeping Tree shed tears so copiously that a small pool formed at its base. Some even claimed to have seen a ghostly figure resembling the Sultan himself, standing beneath the tree's branches, his own tears mingling with those of the ancient plant.

As the Turkish Republic rose from the ashes of the Ottoman Empire, the Weeping Tree became a symbol of a bygone era. For some, it represented a nostalgic link to a glorious past, while for others, it was a reminder of the need to move forward and embrace modernity. Regardless of one's perspective, the tree's legend continued to captivate the imagination of Istanbul's residents and visitors alike.

Over the decades, countless theories have been proposed to explain the tree's unusual behavior. Some argue that its roots have tapped into an underground spring, causing water to seep up through its trunk and branches. Others point to unique atmospheric conditions in that part of the park, suggesting that dew forms more readily on this particular tree due to its location and the surrounding topography.

More fanciful explanations have also gained traction. Some believe that the tree was planted over the grave of an Ottoman mystic, whose spirit infuses the plant with supernatural properties. Others claim that it grew from a seed brought back from Mecca by a sultan, imbuing it with holy power and a deep connection to Islamic history.

· · ·

Whatever the truth behind its tears, the Weeping Tree has become an integral part of Gülhane Park's landscape and Istanbul's folklore. Visitors to the park often seek it out, hoping to witness its legendary weeping for themselves. While daytime sightings are rare, those who venture into the park after dark sometimes report seeing a faint shimmer on the tree's leaves or feeling an inexplicable dampness in the air around it.

The tree has also become a focal point for those who feel a connection to Ottoman history and culture. On significant anniversaries related to the empire's past, small groups can often be found gathered near the tree, sharing stories and memories passed down through generations. Some leave offerings at its base - coins, flowers, or small mementos - as a way of paying respect to the legacy it represents.

For historians and botanists, the Weeping Tree presents an intriguing case study. While most experts dismiss the supernatural aspects of the legend, many find the tree itself worthy of study. Its longevity and apparent health, despite the urban environment and the touch of countless visitors, make it a subject of scientific interest.

The tree's fame has spread beyond Istanbul, featuring in travel guides and documentaries about the city's hidden wonders. It's become a staple of ghost tours and historical walks, with guides weaving its story into broader narratives about the rise and fall of empires and the enduring power of nature.

In recent years, as interest in Ottoman history has experienced a resurgence in Turkey, the Weeping Tree has taken on new significance. It features in historical novels and films set in the late impe-rial period, often as a backdrop for pivotal scenes or as a metaphor for the empire's fading glory. Some contemporary artists have created works inspired by the tree, exploring themes of memory, loss, and the passage of time.

Conservation efforts have also been undertaken to protect the Weeping Tree. While Gülhane Park as a whole is well-maintained, special attention is given to this particular tree. Arborists regularly check its health, and measures have been taken to protect its roots from compaction caused by foot traffic. There's even been talk of installing a discrete irrigation system to ensure the tree continues to "weep" for future generations, though purists argue this would detract from the legend's mystique.

The story of the Weeping Tree has evolved over time, adapting to reflect changing attitudes towards Ottoman history and Turkey's place in the modern world. For some, it remains a symbol of loss and nostalgia for a bygone era. For others, it represents resilience - a living link to the past that continues to thrive in the present.

Interestingly, the legend has also spawned a number of offshoots and related tales. Some claim that on particularly significant nights, the weeping isn't limited to this one tree, but can be observed in other old trees throughout Istanbul. Others insist that the tree's tears have healing properties, leading to occasional gath-erings of people seeking cures for various ailments.

There are even those who believe that the Weeping Tree's tears are not tears at all, but laughter. This interpretation sees the tree not as mourning the past, but as chuckling at the folly of human empires and the ephemeral nature of power. It's a perspective that adds a layer of philosophical depth to the legend, inviting contemplation on the cyclical nature of history and the enduring power of nature.

As Istanbul continues to grow and change, balancing its rich history with the demands of a modern metropolis, the Weeping Tree stands as a silent witness to the city's transformations. It serves as a reminder that even in the midst of a bustling urban landscape, there are still places where magic and mystery can take root.

For the people of Istanbul, whether they believe in its supernatural qualities or not, the Weeping Tree is a cherished part of their city's landscape. It's a living piece of folklore, a natural monument that connects the present to the past in a tangible way. In its gnarled trunk and spreading branches, in the droplets that may or may not be tears, the tree embodies the complex, layered history of Istanbul itself.

As night falls over Gülhane Park and the last visitors make their way to the exits, the Weeping Tree stands in solitude. Perhaps, if one listens closely, they might hear the soft patter of droplets hitting the ground, or catch a glimpse of moisture glistening on a leaf. Or perhaps they'll simply feel a sense of connection to the countless others who have stood in that spot over the decades, wondering at the mysteries held within its ancient bark.

Whether the Weeping Tree truly sheds tears for a lost empire or is simply an unusually moist plane tree, its legend continues to capture the imagination of all who hear it. It stands as a testament to Istanbul's ability to blend the natural and the supernatural, the historical and the mythical, creating stories that resonate across generations and cultures. In the end, the true magic of the Weeping Tree may lie not in any supernatural properties, but in its power to make us pause, reflect, and wonder at the deep connections between nature, history, and the human spirit.

THE SULTAN'S TREASURE

In the sweltering summer of 1933, Istanbul was abuzz with excitement. The city, always a hotbed of rumors and whispers, was alive with talk of buried treasure. It all began when a group of workers, digging the foundations for a new government building near Topkapı Palace, struck something solid with their shovels. As they cleared away the dirt, they uncovered a small, hidden chamber. Inside, glinting in the sunlight that now reached it for the first time in decades, was a hoard of gold coins and priceless artifacts.

.   .   .

Word spread quickly through the narrow streets and bustling markets. The treasure, it was said, belonged to none other than Sultan Abdülhamid II, the last of the great Ottoman rulers. Abdülhamid, known for his paranoia and secretive nature, had reportedly hidden vast amounts of wealth throughout the city during his reign. This discovery, many believed, was just the tip of the iceberg.

The find couldn't have come at a more opportune time. Istanbul, like much of the world, was in the grip of the Great Depression. The promise of hidden riches buried beneath the streets was intoxicating. Almost overnight, the city transformed into a hive of amateur treasure hunters and would-be archaeologists.

People from all walks of life were caught up in the fever. Shopkeepers closed early to go digging in their basements. Families spent weekends exploring abandoned buildings and overgrown lots. Even some of the city's elite could be seen poking around old Ottoman-era mansions, hoping to uncover secret chambers or forgotten vaults.

The authorities tried to maintain order, insisting that any finds be reported and turned over to the state. But in the excitement of the hunt, many chose to keep their activities secret, dreaming of the fortune that might change their lives forever.

One of those caught up in the treasure hunting craze was Mehmet, a young cab driver struggling to make ends meet. He had grown up hearing stories of the Ottoman sultans and their legendary wealth. The discovery near Topkapı Palace ignited his imagination. Every fare he picked up seemed to have a new theory about where the sultan's treasure might be hidden.

Mehmet began spending his free time researching Ottoman history, poring over old maps of the city, and questioning elderly relatives about family legends and local folklore. He became convinced that he could crack the code and find the mother lode of Abdülhamid's hidden wealth.

His search led him to an old hamam in the Sultanahmet district. The bathhouse had been abandoned for years, its once-grand domes now crumbling and overgrown with weeds. Local legend held that it had been a favorite retreat of Abdülhamid II. Mehmet reasoned that if the sultan had hidden treasure anywhere, it would be in a place he knew well and trusted.

For weeks, Mehmet spent his nights exploring the hamam, tapping on walls, and measuring distances between columns, looking for any sign of hidden chambers or secret passageways. His friends thought he had gone mad, but Mehmet was undeterred. He was sure he was on the verge of a great discovery.

Meanwhile, across the city in the ancient district of Eyüp, another treasure hunter was following a different lead. Ayşe, a schoolteacher with a passion for history, had been researching the final days of the Ottoman Empire. She had come across mentions of a loyal servant of Abdülhamid II who had lived in Eyüp. According to the accounts, this servant had been entrusted with safeguarding some of the sultan's personal belongings during the tumultuous period when Abdülhamid was deposed.

. . .

Ayşe tracked down the descendants of this servant, an elderly couple living in a dilapidated Ottoman-era house. At first, they were reluctant to speak with her, but Ayşe's genuine interest in their family history won them over. Over glasses of sweet tea, they shared stories passed down through generations about their ancestor's connection to the sultan.

One tale particularly caught Ayşe's attention. The couple spoke of a room in their house that had been sealed off for as long as anyone could remember. Family lore held that it contained items left in their great-grandfather's care by Abdülhamid himself, never to be opened until the sultan returned to claim them.

With trembling hands, the old man led Ayşe to a section of wall covered by a heavy tapestry. When they pulled it aside, they found the outline of a door, long ago plastered over. Ayşe's heart raced. Could this be the secret chamber she had been searching for?

As news of these potential discoveries spread, the treasure hunting fever in Istanbul reached new heights. The city became a patchwork of digging sites and impromptu archaeological excavations. Some efforts were methodical and careful, while others were haphazard and destructive.

The authorities struggled to keep up. The Ministry of Culture and Tourism issued stern warnings about damaging historical sites and reminded citizens that any artifacts found belonged to the state. But with the allure of untold riches, many chose to ignore these admonitions.

. . .

The treasure hunt also attracted its share of charlatans and con artists. Self-proclaimed psychics offered their services to locate hidden chambers. Fake maps purporting to show the location of the sultan's treasure were sold in back alleys and coffee houses. More than a few gullible treasure hunters found themselves swindled out of their life savings.

As months passed, the initial excitement began to wane. Many amateur diggers, having found nothing but dirt and broken pottery, gave up their quests. But a dedicated core of treasure hunters persisted, convinced that the big discovery was just around the corner.

Mehmet's exploration of the old hamam had yielded no treasure, but it had uncovered something perhaps more valuable. In his meticulous examination of the building, he had discovered ancient frescoes hidden beneath layers of plaster. The find attracted the attention of art historians and archaeologists, leading to a proper excavation and restoration of the site.

Ayşe's sealed room in Eyüp turned out to contain no gold or jewels, but it did hold a trove of historical documents and personal items belonging to Abdülhamid II. These artifacts provided invaluable insights into the final years of the Ottoman Empire, shedding light on a period of history that had long been shrouded in mystery.

As the great treasure hunt of 1933 faded into memory, it left behind a changed city. The experience had awakened in many Istanbulites a newfound appreciation for their city's rich history. The hunt had uncovered not the vast material wealth they had hoped for, but something perhaps more valuable – a deeper connection to their past.

The legacy of the treasure hunt lived on in other ways as well. It inspired a generation of Turkish archaeologists and historians, who approached their work with the same passion and curiosity that had driven the amateur treasure hunters of 1933. In the decades that followed, their professional excavations and research would uncover many real treasures from Istanbul's long and storied past.

The hunt also left its mark on Istanbul's popular culture. Stories of hidden treasures and secret chambers became a staple of local folklore. Novels and films were inspired by the events of 1933, each adding their own embellishments to the tale. Even today, nearly a century later, whispers of undiscovered Ottoman treasures still circulate in the city's tea houses and markets.

For Mehmet and Ayşe, the treasure hunt had been a transformative experience. Mehmet's discovery in the hamam led him to a new career in historical preservation. He never found the gold he had dreamed of, but he did find a calling that brought him satisfaction and respect.

Ayşe's work with the documents found in Eyüp launched her academic career. She became a renowned expert on late Ottoman history, her research shaped by the understanding that sometimes the most valuable historical treasures are not gold or jewels, but the everyday items and personal writings that provide windows into the past.

. . .

As for Sultan Abdülhamid II's fabled treasure, debates continue to this day about how much wealth he actually hid and how much was simply the product of rumor and imagination. Occasional discoveries in Istanbul still spark speculation about lost Ottoman riches, but none have ever matched the excitement of that summer in 1933.

The true treasure of Istanbul, many came to realize, was not buried underground but was all around them – in the city's magnificent architecture, its rich culture, and the stories passed down through generations. The great treasure hunt may not have uncovered vast material wealth, but it had revealed the true value of Istanbul's historical legacy, a treasure that continues to enrich the city and its people to this day.

As the sun sets over the Bosphorus, painting the sky in hues of gold and crimson, one can almost imagine the ghosts of treasure hunters past still searching the city's ancient streets. Their dreams of instant riches may have faded, but the spirit of discovery they awakened continues to inspire those who seek to uncover the many layers of Istanbul's fascinating history.

31

THE TIME-TRAVELING COFFEEHOUSE

In the streets of Beyoğlu, stands a coffeehouse that defies the normal flow of time. From the outside, it appears unremarkable - a weathered wooden door, windows clouded with age, and a faded sign that simply reads "Zaman Kahvesi" or "Time Coffeehouse." But those who venture inside on certain moonlit nights find themselves stepping not just into a quaint café, but into the swirling eddies of history itself.

. . .

The origins of Zaman Kahvesi are shrouded in mystery. Some say it was established during the reign of Suleiman the Magnificent, a gathering place for poets and philosophers. Others insist it came later, in the twilight years of the Ottoman Empire, a haven for revolutionaries and dreamers. What's certain is that the coffee-house has stood witness to centuries of Istanbul's ever-changing story.

The first recorded mention of the coffeehouse's unusual properties dates back to the late 19th century. A British traveler, in a dusty journal found years later, wrote of an extraordinary experience he had while sipping Turkish coffee in a "nondescript establishment off the Grande Rue de Pera" (now İstiklal Avenue). He described overhearing a heated debate about the merits of the printing press - a debate that would have been current two centuries earlier.

At first, the traveler assumed it was some sort of historical reenactment. But as the night wore on and the conversations around him shifted and changed, he realized he was hearing snip-pets of dialogue from various periods in Istanbul's past. Bewil-dered and more than a little frightened, he fled the coffeehouse, convinced he had stumbled into some sort of temporal anomaly.

For decades, similar stories trickled out of Beyoğlu. Patrons would emerge from Zaman Kahvesi with tales of hearing languages long dead, of glimpsing fashions from bygone eras in the mirror behind the bar, of smelling gunpowder and incense mingling with the scent of freshly ground coffee beans. Most were dismissed as the product of overactive imaginations fueled by too much caffeine and nargile smoke.

. . .

But as the years passed and the stories accumulated, a pattern began to emerge. The coffeehouse's time-bending properties seemed to manifest only on certain nights - usually when the moon was full and a particular alignment of stars was visible in the sky above Istanbul. On these nights, those who knew where to look would see a soft, pulsing glow emanating from the windows of Zaman Kahvesi.

One of the coffeehouse's most frequent visitors in recent years is Leyla, a history professor at Istanbul University. She stumbled upon Zaman Kahvesi by accident one foggy evening, seeking shelter from a sudden rainstorm. What she found inside changed her understanding of history forever.

As Leyla sipped her coffee, she became aware of a conversation at the next table. Two men in Ottoman-era clothing were discussing the recent conquest of Constantinople as if it had just happened. Leyla, her academic curiosity overcoming her disbelief, listened intently. The details she overheard about the fall of the Byzantine capital were so vivid, so immediate, that they couldn't possibly be a reenactment.

Just as she was about to interject, the scene shifted. The Ottoman gentlemen were gone, replaced by a group of women in 1920s flapper dresses, excitedly whispering about the new Turkish Republic and the reforms of Atatürk. Before Leyla's eyes, the coffeehouse seemed to ripple and change, each wave bringing a new era into focus.

Since that night, Leyla has been a regular at Zaman Kahvesi, meticulously documenting her experiences. She's overheard discussions about the construction of the Hagia Sophia, arguments about the Crimean War, and excited chatter about the first crossing of the Bosphorus Bridge. Each visit brings new insights, filling in gaps in the historical record and providing a level of detail no archive could match.

But Leyla is not the only one who has discovered the coffeehouse's secret. Over the years, a small, eclectic group of regulars has formed - artists seeking inspiration from the past, philosophers pondering the nature of time, and even a quantum physicist trying to unravel the scientific principles behind the temporal anomalies.

One of the most colorful regulars is Ahmet, an elderly gentleman who claims to have been visiting Zaman Kahvesi for over sixty years. With a twinkle in his eye, he recounts how he once shared a table with a young Orhan Pamuk, long before the author's rise to fame. According to Ahmet, Pamuk was deep in conversation with a poet from the 16th century, their discussion about the nature of storytelling spanning centuries.

The current owner of the coffeehouse, a enigmatic woman known only as Madame Zaman, is as mysterious as the establishment itself. Some swear she hasn't aged a day in decades, while others insist she's a different person every time they visit. Madame Zaman neither confirms nor denies the stories about her coffeehouse, simply smiling enigmatically when asked and recommending her special blend of coffee "for those who wish to taste history."

Not all experiences at Zaman Kahvesi are pleasant, however. There are whispered stories of patrons who stayed too long, becoming lost in the currents of time. One tale speaks of a young artist who became so entranced by a conversation with the legendary architect Mimar Sinan that he forgot to leave before dawn. When the morning light touched the coffeehouse, the artist vanished, leaving behind only a sketchbook filled with designs for buildings that would not be constructed for centuries.

The coffeehouse has its skeptics, of course. Many dismiss the stories as urban legends or clever marketing. Some have tried to debunk the myth, spending nights at Zaman Kahvesi with recording equipment and cameras. Strangely, their devices always seem to malfunction on the nights when the time-slips are said to occur.

Despite (or perhaps because of) the controversy, Zaman Kahvesi has become something of a cultural icon in Istanbul. Its influence can be seen in the works of local artists and writers, who draw inspiration from the idea of a place where all of Istanbul's history coexists. Musicians have composed pieces that attempt to capture the sensation of hearing centuries of the city's sounds overlapping and intertwining.

For many Istanbul residents, whether they believe the stories or not, Zaman Kahvesi represents something essential about their city. It's a physical manifestation of the way Istanbul itself seems to exist in multiple time periods simultaneously, where ancient monuments stand alongside modern skyscrapers, and where traditions dating back millennia coexist with cutting-edge technology.

The coffeehouse has also become a pilgrimage site for history enthusiasts and time travel aficionados from around the world. On nights when the temporal phenomena are said to be strongest, a diverse crowd gathers in Zaman Kahvesi. Scholars sit next to wide-eyed tourists, all hoping to catch a glimpse through the veils of time.

Some come with specific questions about historical events, hoping to overhear a firsthand account that might settle long-standing debates. Others simply want to immerse themselves in the atmosphere, to feel the weight of centuries pressing in around them as they sip their coffee.

The effect of Zaman Kahvesi extends beyond its walls. Those who have experienced its time-slipping properties often report a changed perspective on the city. They begin to see echoes of the past in everyday life - a gesture, a phrase, a custom that has survived through the centuries. Istanbul, always a city of layers, becomes even richer and more complex through the lens of the coffeehouse's patrons.

As word of Zaman Kahvesi has spread, it has faced its share of challenges. Developers, eager to modernize Beyoğlu, have made offers to buy the property. Government officials, concerned about the implications of a temporal anomaly in the heart of the city, have attempted to regulate or shut down the establishment. But somehow, Zaman Kahvesi endures, protected perhaps by the very temporal distortions that make it unique.

For now, the Time Coffeehouse remains a constant in a ever-changing city, a place where the past is never truly past and where the rich tapestry of Istanbul's history is always on display. Those who know its secret continue to gather on moonlit nights, ordering coffee from an ageless proprietor and settling in to eavesdrop on the centuries.

.   .   .

As the murmur of countless conversations from across time fills the air, mingling with the rich aroma of Turkish coffee, patrons of Zaman Kahvesi are reminded of a fundamental truth about Istanbul: in this city, history is not just something to be studied in books or observed in museums. It's a living, breathing entity, as vital and immediate as the present moment. And sometimes, if you know where to look and how to listen, you can hear its heartbeat in the most unexpected places - like a small, unassuming coffeehouse where time itself comes to take a break and enjoy a cup of coffee.

32

THE DISAPPEARING DIPLOMAT

On a crisp autumn morning in 1967, the staff at the Soviet Consulate in Istanbul arrived to find the office of Dmitri Kovlov, their senior cultural attaché, eerily empty. His desk was cleared, his personal effects gone, and a half-empty cup of coffee sat cold on the windowsill. Kovlov, a fixture in Istanbul's diplomatic circles for the past five years, had vanished without a trace.

. . .

The disappearance sent shockwaves through the diplomatic community. Kovlov wasn't just any bureaucrat; he was a rising star in the Soviet foreign service, known for his charm, his impeccable Turkish, and his deep connections within Istanbul's cultural elite. His sudden absence triggered a flurry of activity on both sides of the Cold War divide.

Soviet officials, fearing defection or foul play, launched an internal investigation. The KGB dispatched a team to Istanbul, turning the consulate upside down in search of clues. Meanwhile, Turkish authorities, caught between their NATO allies and the need to maintain relations with the Soviet Union, found themselves in a delicate position.

As days turned into weeks with no sign of Kovlov, rumors began to circulate. Some claimed he had been kidnapped by Turkish ultra-nationalists. Others whispered that he had fled with a lover, abandoning his career and family for a romantic escapade. The more conspiracy-minded suggested that Kovlov had been a double agent, eliminated by his own government when his treachery was discovered.

The truth, as is often the case in the shadowy world of espionage, was far more complex.

Unbeknownst to his Soviet colleagues and even his own family, Dmitri Kovlov was not who he claimed to be. His real name was David Cohen, and he was one of the CIA's most valuable assets in Turkey. For over a decade, Cohen had lived a double life, feeding crucial information about Soviet activities in the region back to his handlers in Langley.

. . .

Cohen's journey to becoming Dmitri Kovlov began in the early 1950s. Born to Russian-Jewish immigrants in New York, he showed an early aptitude for languages and a fascination with international affairs. The CIA, always on the lookout for talented recruits, approached him during his final year at Columbia University.

The plan was ambitious and risky. Cohen would be given a new identity as a Soviet citizen, complete with an elaborate backstory and meticulously forged documents. After years of intensive training in Russian language, culture, and Soviet bureaucratic procedures, he would be inserted into the Soviet foreign service through a complex series of manipulations and planted evidence.

The operation was a resounding success. "Dmitri Kovlov" rose through the ranks, his American handlers marveling at his ability to maintain his cover. By the time he was posted to Istanbul in 1962, Cohen was providing invaluable intelligence on Soviet strategies in the Middle East and the Eastern Mediterranean.

Istanbul proved to be the perfect posting for Cohen. The city's position as a crossroads between East and West made it a hotbed of espionage activity. Cohen's role as cultural attaché gave him the perfect cover to move freely in diverse circles, from artist gatherings to academic conferences, all while gathering information and making connections.

But in the summer of 1967, everything changed. A routine counterintelligence sweep by the KGB had uncovered discrepancies in Kovlov's background. As Soviet investigators began to close in, Cohen's CIA handlers realized his cover was about to be blown.

. . .

The extraction plan was put into motion with dizzying speed. On the night of September 14, Cohen attended a diplomatic reception at the Italian Consulate. Amid the clinking of glasses and polite conversation, he slipped away to the restroom. There, he met with a CIA operative disguised as a waiter, who provided him with a new set of clothes and forged Turkish identification papers.

While the party continued upstairs, Cohen exited through a back door into a narrow alley where a car was waiting. By the time his absence was noted at the reception, he was already on his way to a safe house on the outskirts of Istanbul.

For the next 48 hours, Cohen remained hidden as CIA operatives worked to smuggle him out of the country. It was a race against time, with KGB agents scouring the city and Turkish police on high alert. Finally, in the early hours of September 17, Cohen was smuggled aboard a U.S. military transport plane disguised as a member of the crew.

As Kovlov's colleagues at the Soviet Consulate were just beginning to notice his absence, David Cohen was touching down on American soil for the first time in over 15 years.

The fallout from Cohen's extraction was immediate and far-reaching. The Soviet Union, realizing they had been duped, launched a massive security review, paranoia spreading through their foreign service like wildfire. Diplomats were recalled, security protocols overhauled, and countless careers ended under suspicion of American infiltration.

· · ·

In Turkey, the disappearance caused diplomatic tensions. The Soviet Union accused Turkey of complicity in Kovlov's vanishing act, while the Turkish government protested its innocence, genuinely unaware of the CIA operation that had unfolded on their soil.

For years, the mystery of Dmitri Kovlov's disappearance remained unsolved in the public eye. It became the subject of books and articles, each proposing new theories but never quite cracking the truth. It wasn't until the end of the Cold War, when CIA archives began to be declassified, that the full story came to light.

David Cohen, meanwhile, found adjusting to life back in the United States challenging. After years of living as Dmitri Kovlov, he struggled with his identity. The CIA provided him with a new name and background, setting him up with a quiet job in academia. But the habits of a lifetime of espionage were hard to break.

In Istanbul, the legend of the disappearing diplomat lived on. Tour guides would point out the former Soviet Consulate building to visitors, recounting the tale of the vanishing cultural attaché. In the city's many coffeehouses, older patrons still sometimes debate the various theories, unaware that the truth is far stranger than any of their speculations.

The case of Dmitri Kovlov/David Cohen became a textbook example in intelligence circles of both the potential and the dangers of deep-cover operations. It highlighted the human cost of espionage, the blurring of identities, and the complex web of international relations that could be shaken by a single individual's actions.

.   .   .

For Istanbul, the incident underscored the city's unique position as a crucible of international intrigue. Straddling Europe and Asia, it had long been a city where East met West, where empires clashed and cultures mingled. In the 20th century, this made it a natural theater for the shadow wars of espionage.

The Kovlov affair also left a lasting mark on Istanbul's diplomatic community. For years afterward, diplomats posted to the city found themselves under increased scrutiny, both from their host country and their own governments. The ghost of the man who vanished continued to haunt embassy cocktail parties and consular offices.

In the decades since Cohen's extraction, Istanbul has continued to evolve, but it remains a city of secrets and stories. The tale of the disappearing diplomat is now just one thread in the complex tapestry of legends that make up the city's modern mythology.

Visitors to Istanbul today might pass by the old Soviet Consulate building without realizing its significance. The diplomats and spies who once walked its halls have long since moved on, replaced by new players in the ever-shifting game of international relations. But for those who know where to look, the echoes of that September night in 1967 can still be felt.

In a small café not far from where Dmitri Kovlov attended his last diplomatic function, an old man sometimes sits, nursing a cup of Turkish coffee and watching the world go by. Some say he bears a striking resemblance to photos of the vanished diplomat, aged by the years. Others insist he's just another Istanbul pensioner, whiling away his retirement.

.   .   .

Whether he's a ghost from the past or simply a figment of the city's imagination, the man serves as a reminder that in Istanbul, the line between history and legend is often blurred. In this city where continents meet, where empires have risen and fallen, stories like that of the disappearing diplomat continue to capture the imagination, a testament to Istanbul's enduring place at the crossroads of global intrigue.

33

THE SPY IN THE HAREM

In the opulent halls of Topkapi Palace, where whispers carried the weight of empires, a most unlikely spy wove her way through the intricate tapestry of Ottoman court life. Aimée du Buc de Rivéry, a French noblewoman turned captive, became an enigmatic figure in the Sultan's harem, her true allegiances known only to a select few.

. . .

Aimée's journey from the sun-drenched shores of Martinique to the sequestered world of the Ottoman harem reads like a fantastical tale. Born into a wealthy plantation-owning family in 1776, she was sent to France for her education, as was common for girls of her social standing. It was on her return voyage in 1788, at the tender age of 13, that fate intervened in the form of Barbary pirates.

The pirate attack was swift and merciless. Aimée, along with the ship's other passengers, was taken captive. While many of her fellow travelers faced grim futures in the slave markets of North Africa, Aimée's beauty and refined manners caught the attention of the pirate captain. Sensing an opportunity for a substantial ransom, he decided to present her as a gift to the Ottoman Sultan, Abdulhamid I.

Upon her arrival in Istanbul, Aimée found herself thrust into the mysterious world of the harem. The initial shock and terror of her captivity gradually gave way to a keen sense of observation. She quickly realized that the harem was not merely a place of pleasure, but a complex political ecosystem, where power was wielded through whispers, alliances, and carefully guarded secrets.

Aimée's intelligence and adaptability served her well. She learned Turkish and Arabic with remarkable speed, and her natural charm helped her navigate the treacherous waters of harem politics. Within a few years, she had caught the eye of the new Sultan, Selim III, a reformist ruler with a fascination for European culture.

It was during this time that Aimée, now known by her Ottoman name Nakşidil, began her covert activities. Using her position as a favored concubine, she gathered information about the inner workings of the Ottoman court, the Sultan's plans for modernizing the empire, and the various factions vying for power.

Her method of passing this intelligence to French agents in Istanbul was ingenious in its simplicity. Aimée would embroider coded messages into intricate tapestries, which were then sold in the Grand Bazaar. French operatives, posing as merchants, would purchase these tapestries, decoding the hidden information upon their return to the embassy.

The information Aimée provided proved invaluable to France during a period of complex diplomatic maneuvering. As Napoleon sought to expand his influence in the Mediterranean, insights into Ottoman military capabilities, diplomatic leanings, and internal power struggles gave French negotiators a significant advantage.

However, Aimée's role as a spy was complicated by her growing attachment to her adopted home. As years passed, she found herself torn between loyalty to her French heritage and a genuine affection for the Ottoman Empire and its people. This internal conflict was further complicated when she gave birth to a son, Mahmud, who would later become Sultan Mahmud II.

Aimée's influence extended beyond mere intelligence gathering. She became a key advocate for modernization within the Ottoman court, encouraging Sultan Selim III's reforms and later guiding her son Mahmud II towards a more progressive vision for the empire. Her unique perspective as both an insider and outsider allowed her to bridge cultural gaps and foster understanding between East and West.

. . .

The extent of Aimée's espionage activities remained a closely guarded secret for decades. It wasn't until the mid-19th century, long after her death, that rumors began to circulate about the French woman in the Sultan's harem who had played a crucial role in shaping Ottoman-French relations.

These rumors were fueled by the discovery of a series of letters in the French diplomatic archives, written in a code that took years to decipher. The letters, signed only with the initial 'A', provided detailed accounts of Ottoman military strength, court intrigues, and policy debates that could only have come from someone deep within the imperial household.

As news of Aimée's double life spread, it captured the imagination of both Europeans and Ottomans. In Paris, she was hailed as a heroic daughter of France, bravely serving her nation from within the heart of a rival power. In Istanbul, opinions were more divided. Some saw her as a traitor who had betrayed the trust of her adopted home, while others admired her cunning and ability to navigate between two worlds.

The legend of Aimée du Buc de Rivéry, the spy in the harem, grew with each retelling. Books were written, plays were performed, and countless theories were proposed about the true extent of her influence. Some even suggested that she had been the real power behind the Ottoman throne for decades, shaping imperial policy from the shadows.

In Istanbul, the story of Aimée became intertwined with other tales of the city's cosmopolitan past. Tour guides would point out spots in Topkapi Palace where she supposedly met with French agents, or where she whispered crucial secrets into the ear of Sultan Selim III. The tapestries in the palace took on new significance, with visitors scrutinizing every stitch for hidden messages.

The tale of the French spy in the harem also sparked a renewed interest in the role of women in Ottoman court life. Historians began to re-examine the harem not just as a secluded world of pleasure, but as a complex political and social institution where women wielded significant, if informal, power.

Aimée's story resonated particularly strongly with the women of Istanbul. In a society still grappling with questions of women's rights and roles, she became a symbol of female empowerment and cunning. Young girls were told bedtime stories about the clever French woman who outwitted sultans and spies alike.

In the grand coffeehouses of Beyoğlu, where Istanbul's intellectuals gathered to debate politics and culture, the case of Aimée du Buc de Rivéry became a popular topic of discussion. Was she a hero or a traitor? A victim of circumstance or a master manipulator? The debates would often last long into the night, fueled by strong Turkish coffee and the enduring mystery of the woman herself.

The impact of Aimée's espionage activities extended far beyond her lifetime. The information she provided played a crucial role in shaping French policy towards the Ottoman Empire during a period of significant geopolitical shifts. Her insights into the strengths and weaknesses of the Ottoman state influenced diplomatic strategies that would have long-lasting effects on the balance of power in the Mediterranean.

. . .

Moreover, Aimée's dual role as both spy and advocate for modernization left a complex legacy. The reforms she championed, first through Sultan Selim III and later through her son Mahmud II, set the Ottoman Empire on a path of Westernization that would fundamentally alter its character in the decades to come.

Today, visitors to Istanbul can still feel the echoes of Aimée's extraordinary life. In the hushed rooms of Topkapi Palace, one can almost imagine the rustle of silk as she moved through the harem, her mind cataloging secrets to be woven into her next tapestry. In the Grand Bazaar, among the stalls selling intricate textiles, the ghost of her ingenious communication method lingers.

The story of Aimée du Buc de Rivéry, the spy in the harem, serves as a reminder of Istanbul's long history as a city of secrets and intrigue. It speaks to the complex interplay of cultures, the hidden power of women in seemingly restrictive societies, and the enduring allure of a well-told tale of espionage.

As the sun sets over the Bosphorus and the calls to prayer echo across the city, one can't help but wonder what other secrets Istanbul holds. In this city where East meets West, where empires have risen and fallen, stories like Aimée's remind us that truth is often stranger – and more captivating – than fiction. The spy in the harem may be long gone, but her legend lives on, a testament to the enduring mystery and allure of Istanbul.